# WITH JESUS
# TO THE CROSS

A Lenten Guide on the ................gs:

## Year B

## A Catholic Guide for Small Groups

**the evangelical Catholic**
*forming disciples. training leaders.*

the**WORD**
among us®
*press*

Published by The Word Among Us Press
7115 Guilford Drive, Suite 100
Frederick, Maryland 21704
www.wau.org

22 21 20 19 18  1 2 3 4 5

Nihil obstat:    The Reverend Michael Morgan, J.D., J.C.L.
                 Censor Librorum
                 November 8, 2017

Imprimatur:      + Most Reverend Felipe J. Estévez, S.T.D
                 Bishop of St. Augustine
                 November 8, 2017

ISBN:  978-1-59325-325-7
eISBN: 978-1-59325-502-2

Unless other noted, Scripture texts are taken from the Catholic Edition of the
Revised Standard Version Bible, © 1965, 1966 by the Division of Christian
Education of the National Council of the Churches of Christ in the United States of
America. Used with permission. All rights reserved.

Scripture passages marked "NRSV" are taken from New Revised Standard Version
Bible: Catholic Edition, copyright © 1989, 1993 National Council of the Churches
of Christ in the United States of America.
Used by permission. All rights reserved worldwide.

Excerpts from the English translation of the *Catechism of the Catholic Church* in the
United States of America ©1994, United States Catholic
Conference of Catholic Bishops, Inc.—Libreria Editrice Vaticana.

Cover design by David Crosson
Cover image: Compassion I . 1897.
William-Adolphe Bouguereau (1825-1905)
Location: Musee d'Orsay, Paris, France
Photo Credit: © RMN-Grand Palais/Art Resource, NY

Made and printed in the United States of America

Library of Congress Control Number: 2017958190

# Contents

# Introduction

Behold, now is the acceptable time; behold, now is the day of salvation.

(2 Corinthians 6:2)

How much of life we put off!

> "I'll organize that closet someday . . ."
>
> "Tomorrow I'll start a diet . . ."
>
> "I'll quit smoking once I'm past this stressful time . . ."
>
> "I'll repair that _____ when work isn't so busy . . ."

How many people do you know who never quit smoking, never lose weight, never fix things long broken and unattended?

Isn't this true of everyone? We all put off what we know we could and should do.

And don't we do the same thing with God?

> "I'll pray regularly once the kids are in school, once they're at college, once they're grown up . . ."
>
> "I'll make a confession another time . . ."
>
> "When I'm not so tired from work, I'll make time to read the Scriptures . . ."

Our hearts may be the thing long broken and unattended, but we don't go to the healer, Jesus, the only one who can help us.

As pressing as the physical parts of life are—health, order, home—how much more important are our supernatural lives! God is love, but how can we experience his love without a relationship with him through Jesus, the one God sent to save us?

God shows us his love within the intimacy that comes through daily time with him, just as it does between people. If we never spend that time, if we have never known the supernatural kindness, generosity, and forgiveness of God, how can we ever hope to be kind, generous, and forgiving toward ourselves or others? How can God help us to grow beyond arrogance, rudeness, self-seeking, or anger? That's what it takes to bear with one another, overcome pride, and become patient—all the things St. Paul described as love in his letter to the new believers in Corinth. Even hope depends on love, and who can live without hope (1 Corinthians 13:1-13)?

If God really so loved the world that he sent Jesus to save us, don't you want that love, no matter the cost? Doesn't love always need to move from our heads to our hearts to be love at all?

It is this movement of your heart that God wants at Lent, not a sacrifice of chocolate or any mere "demonstration" of faith. "'Rend your hearts and not your garments.' Return to the LORD, your God" (Joel 2:13).

"Behold, *now* is the acceptable time; behold, now is the day of salvation" (2 Corinthians 6:2)—not someday, *now*.

The Church proclaims these readings every Ash Wednesday to remind us of what we too often neglect. Because we are human beings, the demands of the physical world will always seem more pressing than those of our souls. We need this season to prompt us to put God and our relationship with Jesus at the top of our "to do" lists. We need Lent to inspire us to "rend our hearts."

*With Jesus to the Cross* can help you stop thinking, "I *ought* to do something for Lent; I *want* to do something," and instead actually *do* something. Gather a small group of friends, or other parishioners if you belong to a church, or read each session by yourself and use the questions to reflect on the upcoming Sunday readings. Find why they matter to you, *personally,* to the needs and challenges you experience in your own life. God is always trying to say something to you. Reflecting on the Scriptures is the easiest way to hear him. That's why *lectio divina*, prayerful consideration of the Bible, is the time-honored practice for the personal prayer of Christians.

If you're in a small group, praying together and encouraging one another to daily prayer will help you love Jesus more and follow him closely—even to the cross.

Christians believe that the person of Jesus of Nazareth shows us God the Father in a way we can see and understand, because Jesus is God the Son incarnate, living among us as one of us. He is the "light of the world" (John 8:12); without him, we are in darkness about God's love for us and his desire for a relationship with us. Talking to God and prayerfully reading Scripture bring Jesus' light into every part of our lives. It makes us Jesus' disciples, or God's "students," the original meaning of the word "disciple." "If you continue in my word, you are truly my disciples, and you will know the truth, and the truth will make you free" (John 8:31-32). Christ, who is the light of the world, shows you things as they really are, revealing the lies that you are not good enough, smart enough, thin enough, strong enough. Jesus shows you the truth: that we are beloved children of God.

Use this guide to reflect on the words and actions of Jesus and his earliest followers, and you can experience the truth he proclaimed: God's kingdom is indeed "at hand" (Mark 1:15). It's so close to you because it comes through Jesus, who is always waiting for us: "I am with you always, to the close of the age" (Matthew 28:20).

Dive into the Scriptures using this book during Lent, and talk to God through the weekly guides. God can bring forth a great harvest in your life through these practices. Jesus said the word becomes a seed planted in our hearts when we hear it, one that can bring forth a crop thirty, sixty, even one hundredfold (Mark 4:20).

But it's up to you to be the receptive soil where the seed can germinate and take root. Be faithful to a small group or weekly personal reading and to considering the questions. Between meetings or reading, allow God to water and tend the soil of your soul by following the prayer suggestions. Fasting and almsgiving, the other Lenten practices, will fertilize these seeds as nothing else can. When Holy Week comes, let the field of your heart be drenched in the blood of the Lamb and warmed by the resurrection of the Son on Easter. Your life will be transformed.

Now is the acceptable time. Now is the moment of salvation. Don't miss it!

# How to Use This Small Group Guide

Welcome to *With Jesus to the Cross: Year B*, a small group guide to help you know Jesus of Nazareth more deeply and understand more fully what his death and resurrection mean in your life.

## Weekly Sessions

The weekly sessions use the Sunday Mass readings for Lent to help you enter into the mystery of Christ's life, suffering, and resurrection, the source of our salvation.

Each session includes written opening and closing prayers, the Scripture passage or passages for the coming Sunday, questions for discussion on the Scriptures, ideas for action, and prayer prompts to carry you through the week. Sometimes excerpts from saints, popes, or other great teachers are included that shed light on the message of the gospel.

We recommend that groups meet for the first time socially the week before Lent begins. Books can be distributed or sold at this first meeting, or information can be provided for purchase online. During the week of Ash Wednesday, reflect on the readings for the First Sunday of Lent. Meet weekly until Palm Sunday. We suggest that you don't schedule a meeting during Holy Week. Instead, attend all the Triduum services (Holy Thursday, the Mass of the Lord's Supper, Good Friday, and the Easter Vigil on Saturday night when the Church baptizes new believers). The questions on the Easter readings are designed to be discussed after Easter, not before, so meet again the week after Easter to share your experience of our high holy days.

The sessions in this guide are self-contained. If you or a friend attends for the first time in Week 3, there will be no need to "catch up." Anyone can dive right into the discussion that week with the rest of the group. As with Lent, instead of building sequentially, the sessions deepen thematically, helping you engage more with Jesus and the cross little by little.

The more you take notes, jot down ideas or questions, underline verses in your Bible (if you bring one to your small group, which we recommend!), and refer back to the sessions of previous weeks, the more God has the opportunity to speak to you through the discussion and the ideas he places in your heart. As with any endeavor, the more you put in, the more you get back.

The best way to take advantage of each week's discussion is to carry the theme into your life by following the suggestions in the "Connection to the Cross This Week" section. These prayer prompts will allow Jesus to enlighten your heart and mind on both the challenges of Lent and the joy of the resurrection. If you're discussing the readings with a small group, the facilitator will give you the chance to share experiences from the previous week and talk about the recommendations for the upcoming week during each session.

Each weekly session includes Scripture passages for meditation on the theme of the Sunday readings for that week as well as the daily Mass readings for the coming week. You can find these in your Bible online (biblegateway.com, usccb.org, and other sites), or you can use any of the popular free apps that feature the daily Mass readings, such as Laudate, iMissal, and iBreviary. The entire New American Bible is available at the US Conference of Catholic Bishops' website, usccb.org, as well as the daily readings, including an audio version (http://usccb.org/bible/readings-audio.cfm).

## Appendices

Helpful appendices for both participants and facilitators sup-
plement the weekly materials. Appendices A through D are for
participants, and Appendices E through G are for group facilitators. Prior to your first group meeting, please read Appendix A,
"Small Group Discussion Guide." These guidelines will help every
person in the group set a respectful tone that creates the space
for encountering Christ together.

This small group will differ from other discussion groups you may
have experienced. Is it a lecture? No. A book club? No. Appendix
A will help you understand what this small group is and how you
can help seek a "Spirit-led" discussion. Every member is responsi-
ble for the quality of the group dynamics. This appendix will help
you fulfill your role as a supportive and involved group member.

Appendix B is a resource to enhance and deepen your relationship with Jesus. It encourages you to take the "1% Challenge":
pray at least fifteen minutes each day. That may sound like a lot,
but this appendix also provides a step-by-step guide on how to
spend the time.

Appendix C provides a modified version of an extended meditation by St. Ignatius Loyola, the founder of the Jesuit order. The
"Connection to the Cross This Week" section for the Fourth Sunday of Lent encourages you to use this appendix during the week
to explore your connection to Christ.

In Appendix D, you will find a guide to the Sacrament of Reconciliation, commonly known as Confession. This sacrament bridges
the distance we might feel from God that can come from a variety
of causes, including unrepented sin. The Church encourages Catholics to receive this sacrament each Lent, but it is tremendously

helpful to receive it even more frequently. If you want to grow closer to Jesus and experience great peace, the Sacrament of Reconciliation is the fast track to get there. This appendix will help alleviate any anxiety by leading you through the steps of preparing for and going to Confession. It also gives suggestions for online resources that provide a way to look at your interior life, traditionally called an "examination of conscience."

While Appendices A through D are important for small group participants and facilitators alike, Appendices E through G support the facilitators in their role. A facilitator is not a teacher. His or her role is to buoy the conversation, encourage fruitful group discussion, and tend to the group dynamics.

Appendix E provides guidance and best practices for facilitating a small group successfully, and includes recommendations for any difficult group dynamics that could arise. You will find guidelines on what makes a group work: building genuine friendships, calling for the Holy Spirit to be the group's true facilitator, and seeking joy together.

Appendix F takes the facilitator from the general to the specific, providing detailed leader notes for each session of *With Jesus to the Cross*. Read these notes four or five days before each group meeting. The notes will help you prepare for each session by providing a "heads up" on the content and issues that pertain to discussing these particular Scripture passages.

Facilitators should read Appendix G well in advance of the first meeting. It has the guidance you need to lead prayer and encourage participation in prayer by group members. While the material in each session includes a suggested prayer, this is only support material. It's far better for the group spiritually to pray in their own words. Appendix G will help the facilitator make that happen.

Learning this skill is important. To have a relationship with God, we all need to talk to Jesus in our own words. Closing with extemporaneous prayer is an invaluable way to seal the time you have spent together by offering up the discoveries, questions, sorrows, and joys of your conversation. Appendix G will help leaders guide the group from awkward beginnings to a deepening experience of relationship with God.

Appendix G will also help the facilitator bring the "Connection to the Cross This Week" section into the discussion for each session. It provides concrete suggestions on how to encourage and support group members in their personal engagement with the topics discussed. The facilitator plays a key role in helping participants allow Jesus to become more and more the center of their lives.

Enjoy the adventure!

Sunday of Lent

# A Time to Change

The Spirit immediately
drove him out into the
wilderness.

—Mark 1:12

Praying together in your own words can be more natural than reading a prayer together. Something simple and brief would be fine. You can ask the Lord's blessing on your time together or ask the Holy Spirit to guide your conversation, or you can just thank God for gathering you together to discuss the Lenten Scriptures. Begin and end the prayer with the Sign of the Cross, and you're ready to begin!

Share a prayer of the Church that relates to the topic of this session by having one person slowly read aloud the prayer on the opposite page while the others pray along silently in their hearts. This is an adaptation of the ancient Lenten Prayer of St. Ephrem the Syrian.[1]

[1] Adapted from "Lenten Prayer of St. Ephrem the Syrian," Greek Orthodox Archdiocese of America, https://www.goarch.org/-/lenten-prayer-of-st-ephrem-the-syrian.

**In the name of the Father, and of the Son, and of the Holy Spirit.**

O Lord and Master of our lives,
keep from us the spirit of indifference and discouragement,
lust for power and idle chatter.

Instead, grant to us, your servants, the spirit of
wholeness of being,
humble-mindedness, patience, and love.

O Lord and King, grant us the grace to be aware of our sins
and not to judge our brothers and sisters;
for you are blessed now and forever.

**Amen.**

1. Has anyone ever taken a trip or made a retreat that had a significant impact on your life? Would someone be willing to share about that?

Ask one person to read the Scripture passage aloud.

# Genesis 9:8-15

8 Then God said to Noah and to his sons with him, 9 "Behold, I establish my covenant with you and your descendants after you, 10 and with every living creature that is with you, the birds, the cattle, and every beast of the earth with you, as many as came out of the ark. 11 I establish my covenant with you, that never again shall all flesh be cut off by the waters of a flood, and never again shall there be a flood to destroy the earth." 12 And God said, "This is the sign of the covenant which I make between me and you and every living creature that is with you, for all future generations: 13 I set my bow in the cloud, and it shall be a sign of the covenant between me and the earth. 14 When I bring clouds over the earth and the bow is seen in the clouds, 15 I will remember my covenant which is between me and you and every living creature of all flesh; and the waters shall never again become a flood to destroy all flesh."

1. Can anyone briefly summarize why God told Noah to build the ark?

2. What are some of the emotions Noah and his family may have felt during the flood?

3. Does anyone know what a covenant is? What do you think it involves?

4. Once they received this covenant shown in the rainbow, how do you think Noah and his family would have described the attributes of God?

5. How does considering the experience of Noah and his family add to your understanding of God's relationship with us?

6. Can you think of ways to apply this story of the flood and the covenant to your own spiritual life? Have you ever felt that you were overwhelmed, as Noah was by the flood, and that God made something beautiful from that time?

Ask one person to read the Scripture passage aloud.

# Mark 1:12-15

[12] The Spirit immediately drove him out into the wilderness. [13] And he was in the wilderness forty days, tempted by Satan; and he was with the wild beasts; and the angels ministered to him.

[14] Now after John was arrested, Jesus came into Galilee, preaching the gospel of God, [15] and saying, "The time is fulfilled, and the kingdom of God is at hand; repent, and believe in the gospel."

7. According to Mark's Gospel, why did Jesus go into the wilderness (verse 12)?

8. What did Jesus do after his time in the wilderness, and what do his actions and words mean for you, personally?

9. Lent is forty days (excluding Sundays). Like the flood, the desert or wilderness can be understood as a symbol for our interior lives—for example, a time of purification or seeking. What would it mean for you to go into the desert wilderness this Lent? How would you set about doing that?

10. The wild beasts are unique to the Gospel of Mark's description of Jesus' forty days in the wilderness. (Matthew and Luke tell the longer story of the satanic temptations.) If we understand the wild beasts symbolically, what do you think yours would be? *(Pause.)* Would someone be willing to share?

Time rarely allows for discussion of all three readings at small groups. On one day before the First Sunday of Lent, think or pray about this short second reading from 1 Peter. The questions will help you meditate on the passage to find what God has to say to you through it.

# 1 Peter 3:18-22

[18] For Christ also died for sins once for all, the righteous for the unrighteous, that he might bring us to God, being put to death in the flesh but made alive in the spirit; [19] in which he went and preached to the spirits in prison, [20] who formerly did not obey, when God's patience waited in the days of Noah, during the building of the ark, in which a few, that is, eight persons, were saved through water. [21] Baptism, which corresponds to this, now saves you, not as a removal of dirt from the body but as an appeal to God for a clear conscience, through the resurrection of Jesus Christ, [22] who has gone into heaven and is at the right hand of God, with angels, authorities, and powers subject to him.

1. What does verse 18 say that Christ did?

In this passage, St. Peter taught Christians in the still very young Church that the God to whom Jesus wants to bring us, his Father in heaven, is the same God of Noah in the Hebrew Scriptures. St. Peter explains the mysterious power of our baptismal waters to bring newness of life, not just when we received the sacrament, but throughout our entire lives. Though we still fail and struggle, Catholics believe that through the sacramental grace of Baptism, we can seek "a clear conscience," and that this comes to us "through the resurrection of Jesus Christ" (verse 21).

2. Do you feel that when you've experienced a clear conscience, it came to you in some way through "the resurrection of Jesus Christ"?

3. What does St. Peter's teaching mean for you, personally? Pray about this. Ask Jesus to show you what your baptism means.

On other days this week, choose one or two of the following suggestions on the next page that appeal to you. Plan when you will do it by putting it on your calendar, and then commit to following through. This may sound excessive, but scheduling a specific time to do something helps us to accomplish our goals. Can you think of anything you accomplish without first planning for it and then committing time to do it? Prayer is the same, only it's even *more* important! Talking to Jesus connects us to God, the source of everything real and good! Scheduling will help you do one or two extra things this week to draw closer to Jesus and begin or build your relationship with him. For help meditating on Scripture, see Appendix B, "A Guide to Seeking God in Prayer and Scripture."

- MOST STRONGLY RECOMMENDED: Spend time praying with the daily readings this week. The Church chose them for Lent very intentionally to lead you into deeper conversion. Nothing will draw you into the saving mystery of Jesus' death and resurrection as spending time with him by prayerfully reading the Scriptures and talking to God about them. You will find the Mass readings listed on the opposite page and at the end of every chapter. Search "daily Mass readings" on the Internet to have them with you on a device whenever and wherever you need them. (The USCCB website provides the daily readings in a convenient format, and you can listen to them read aloud as well.)

- Appendix B describes *lectio divina*, a Scripture prayer method from the ancient Church helpful for hearing God speak into our hearts. This practice will enrich and challenge you and bring comfort into your life.

- Write St. Ephrem's prayer, or one or two lines from it, on a note card and tape it to your bathroom mirror or your car dashboard. Let this remind you to pray it every day this week so that the saint's words can inspire you to be faithful to your spiritual goals for Lent.

- Go to a daily Mass this week. Let it be something of a journey into the wilderness of God and away from the busyness of your day.

## This Week's Mass Readings:

Monday: Lv 19:1-2, 11-18 • Ps 19:8-10, 15 • Mt 25:31-46
Tuesday: Is 55:10-11 • Ps 34:4-7, 16-19 • Mt 6:7-15
Wednesday: Jon 3:1-10 • Ps 51:3-4, 12-13, 18-19 • Lk 11:29-32
Thursday: Esth C:12, 14-16, 23-25 • Ps 138:1-3, 7-8 • Mt 7:7-12
Friday: Ez 18:21-28 • Ps 130:1-8 • Mt 5:20-26
Saturday: Dt 26:16-19 • Ps 119:1-2, 4-5, 7-8 • Mt 5:43-48

Not only do angels minister to Jesus and to us—we can minister to one another! Take turns voicing something for which you need prayer. Ideally, this prayer request would relate to the discussion. (For example, you might feel that Jesus' death and resurrection should have a meaningful role in your life, or you may feel that you need a "new covenant" with God because of past suffering or sin. The possibilities are endless.) But whether it relates to the readings or not, ask for what you really need. The leader will sum up these petitions in a prayer at the end and lift them up to God before closing with the prayer on the opposite page.

Listen closely to people's prayer requests so that you can pray for each other's needs during the week. In that way, you will minister to one another.

**In the Name of the Father, and of the Son, and of the Holy Spirit.**

O Christ Jesus, when all is darkness
and we feel our weakness and helplessness,
give us the sense of your presence,
your love, and your strength.
Help us to have perfect trust
in your protecting love
and strengthening power,
so that nothing may frighten or worry us,
for, living close to you,
we shall see your hand,
your purpose,
your will through all things.[2]

**Amen.**

---

[2] "St. Ignatius of Loyola's Prayer Against Depression," EWTN, https://www.ewtn.com/Devotionals/prayers/StIgnatiusPrayerAgainstDepression.htm.

Sunday of Lent
# A Time to Listen

A cloud overshadowed them, and a voice came out of the cloud, "This is my beloved Son; listen to him."

—Mark 9:7

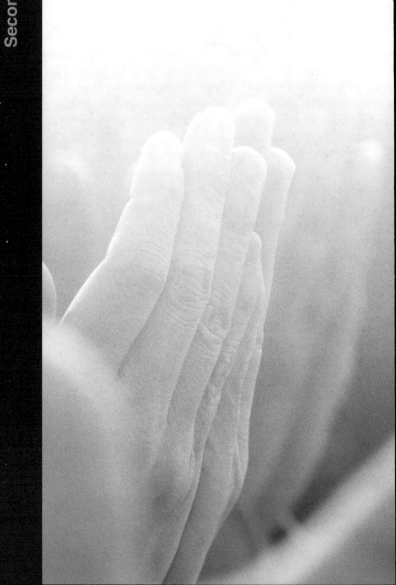

Ask someone to pray in his or her own words, or read the following prayer aloud slowly as others pray along silently.

**In the name of the Father, and of the Son, and of the Holy Spirit.**

Jesus, you ask us to go with you up the mountain.
At the top we stumble on our words;
we look for something to do.

Teach us, Father, how to be still and listen to your Son.
Make our hearts still now;
open them to hear and receive your word—
the Word of Life.

**Amen.**

1. Did anyone find time to read and think about the passage from St. Peter before Mass? How did that affect your experience of Mass?

2. On a scale of 1–10, rate your comfort level with silence with people you know, and then with people you don't know (1 being "I can't stand it"; 10 being "I am completely at ease").

3. If you spend silent time with God, on a scale of 1–10, rate your comfort level during that time.

4. Is this number more similar to your comfort level with someone you know or someone you don't know? What conclusions can you draw?

Ask one person to read the Scripture passage aloud.

# Mark 9:2-10

[2] And after six days Jesus took with him Peter and James and John, and led them up a high mountain apart by themselves; and he was transfigured before them, [3] and his garments became glistening, intensely white, as no fuller on earth could bleach them. [4] And there appeared to them Eli´jah with Moses; and they were talking to Jesus. [5] And Peter said to Jesus, "Master, it is well that we are here; let us make three booths, one for you and one for Moses and one for Eli´jah." [6] For he did not know what to say, for they were exceedingly afraid. [7] And a cloud overshadowed them, and a voice came out of the cloud, "This is my beloved Son; listen to him." [8] And suddenly looking around they no longer saw any one with them but Jesus only.

[9] And as they were coming down the mountain, he charged them to tell no one what they had seen, until the Son of man should have risen from the dead. [10] So they kept the matter to themselves, questioning what the rising from the dead meant.

1. What strikes you from this story? Is there anything you hadn't noticed previously?

2. Peter, James, and John see Jesus in conversation with Moses and Elijah. Recap their responses and other events in the order they occur.

3. How might you explain the reason behind Peter offering to build dwellings for the three of them?

4. What do you think the apostles were "exceedingly afraid" of (verse 6)?

5. Biblical interpreters tell us Moses represents the Law and Elijah the prophets.[1] How does knowing Moses' and Elijah's roles expand your understanding of what is happening in the Transfiguration?

6. St. Thomas Aquinas tells us that the entire Trinity is present on Mount Tabor for the Transfiguration.[2] How would you identify the presence of the Holy Spirit? Does the Holy Spirit's presence add anything to your understanding of the story?

7. God tells the disciples, "This is my beloved Son; listen to him" (verse 7). What does it mean to listen to Christ? How do you do this?

---

[1] *New American Bible, revised edition* footnote for Mark 9:5: "Moses and Elijah represent, respectively, law and prophecy in the Old Testament and are linked to Mount Sinai." http://www.usccb.org/bible/mark/9:35.

[2] "The whole Trinity appeared." St. Thomas Aquinas, quoted in *Catechism of the Catholic Church*, 555.

8. Jesus wants all of us to come away from the crowd so that we can be with him in a quiet place. What hindrances do you face in following him up the mountain? What stops you from going?

9. Have you experienced any obstacles that the disciples experienced on the mountaintop? Fear? Compulsion to speak? To act? (*Pause.*) What are some concrete things you could do to overcome your own obstacles and simply be with God?

If you have time, ask one person to read the following aloud. If not, read it and reflect on the questions before your next meeting.

Thomas Keating is a Trappist monk and priest who, like other monks in his order, follow the Rule of St. Benedict and practice periods of silence. His many books teach about contemplation, a way to deepen our relationship with God through silent prayer.

Jesus in His Divinity is the source of contemplation. When the presence of the Divine is experienced as overwhelming, we are inwardly compelled to contemplate. Such was the situation of the apostles on Mount Tabor when they witnessed the glory of God shining through the humanity of Jesus. They fell on their faces. . . .

Jesus took with him the three disciples who were best prepared to receive the grace of contemplation; that is, the ones who had made the most headway in changing their hearts. God approached them through their senses by means of the vision on the mountain. At first they were overawed and delighted. Peter wanted to remain there forever. Suddenly a cloud covered them, hiding the vision and leaving their senses empty and quiet, yet attentive and alert. The gesture of falling on their faces accurately expressed their state of mind. It was a posture of adoration, gratitude, and love all rolled into one. The voice from heaven awakened their consciousness to the presence of the Spirit, who had always been speaking within them, but whom until then they had never been able to hear. Their interior emptiness was filled with the luminous presence of the divine. At Jesus' touch they returned to their ordinary perceptions and saw him as he was before but with the transformed consciousness of faith. They no longer saw him as a mere human being. Their receptive and active faculties had been unified by the Spirit; the interior and exterior word of God had become one. For those who have attained this consciousness, daily life is a continual and increasing revelation of God. The words they hear in scripture and in the liturgy confirm what they have learned through the prayer that is contemplation.[3]

[3] Thomas Keating, OCSO, *Open Mind, Open Heart* (Rockport: Element, 1992), pp. 16–18.

10. Fr. Keating says that Jesus took the three disciples because they had made the most headway in changing their hearts to receive grace. This implies that God prepares us to receive the graces he wants to give us, and we cooperate with that preparation. Does that seem true to you? What do you do, or could you do, to prepare yourself to encounter God in prayer?

The second reading on Sunday is Romans 8:31-34. Before Sunday, pray over this passage and consider the questions below.

# Romans 8:31-34

[31] If God is for us, who is against us? [32] He who did not spare his own Son but gave him up for us all, will he not also give us all things with him? [33] Who shall bring any charge against God's elect? It is God who justifies; [34] who is to condemn? Is it Christ Jesus, who died, yes, who was raised from the dead, who is at the right hand of God, who indeed intercedes for us?

1. Do you feel that God is "for you"? Talk to Jesus about any feelings and thoughts about this.

2. St. Paul asks, "Who is to condemn?" (verse 34) because Jesus died for you, his follower, so that you would be freed from condemnation and receive new life. Do you condemn yourself? Others? Talk to Jesus about this area of your life. Ask for his help to grow beyond condemnation of yourself and others.

# On two other days before the next meeting:

If you already pray daily, add silence to your prayer. Try resting quietly in the Lord one day this week. Just turn your inward gaze toward God, and keep refocusing every time you notice you're distracted. You will get distracted—even longtime practitioners of silent prayer experience distractions, and every great teacher on prayer says it doesn't matter in the slightest! Parents' hearts swell with joy when their toddler looks at them with eyes full of love, even for a moment or two, before the child's attention jumps to something else. Our Father God loves us the same way! God created our minds; he knows how they dart from one thing to another.

Many techniques can help us sit comfortably in silent prayer. A simple one is to picture your heart as an empty bowl, tilted out toward God, being wordlessly filled by God. Or you could focus on your breathing: pause for a second after you take in air, and pause for another second before you let it out. The word for "spirit" in the Bible is "breath." God breathed life into us. Our lives depend on our breath. Focusing on it allows you to focus on the Spirit and the reality of life itself in that moment.

You may find these suggestions helpful; if not, skip them! But no matter what you do, trust that you're in the presence of God. Jesus said, "I am with you always, to the close of the age" (Matthew 28:20). Believe him!

If you don't already pray daily, try to pray for fifteen minutes—only 1% of your day—on two days this week. If you find the silence challenging, read the Gospel passage for that day (see the list of daily readings on the next page). Think about it. Talk to God about your thoughts, and then rest for a moment or two with God. (For more guidance, see Appendix B, "A Guide to Seeking God in Prayer and Scripture," which explains *lectio divina*, the ancient Christian method of praying with Scripture.) Thank God for the blessings in your life, and close with an Our Father.

## This Week's Mass Readings:

Monday: Dn 9:4-10 • Ps 79:8-9, 11, 13 • Lk 6:36-38

Tuesday: Is 1:10, 16-20 • Ps 50:8-9, 16-17, 21, 23 • Mt 23:1-12

Wednesday: Jer 18:18-20 • Ps 31:5-6, 14-16 • Mt 20:17-28

Thursday: Jer 17:5-10 • Ps 1:1-4, 6 • Lk 16:19-31

Friday: Gn 37:3-4, 12-13, 17-28 • Ps 105:16-21 • Mt 21:33-43, 45-46

Saturday: Mi 7:14-15, 18-20 • Ps 103:1-4, 9-12 • Lk 15:1-3, 11-32

Share your prayer needs first. The leader or someone else can summarize these before closing with the prayer below, or an Our Father.

**In the name of the Father, and of the Son, and of the Holy Spirit.**

Into the silence.
An invitation to the places we keep hidden.
Buried under noise, activity, preoccupation,
there is the quiet place where God waits.
One foot, now another:
descend the stair.

Now, there, in your heart,
breathe the Spirit
who isn't afraid
of your sin,
of your weakness,
of your shame,
but who waits in the very midst of it
to embrace you,
to comfort you,
to burn away
what keeps you apart.

**Amen.**

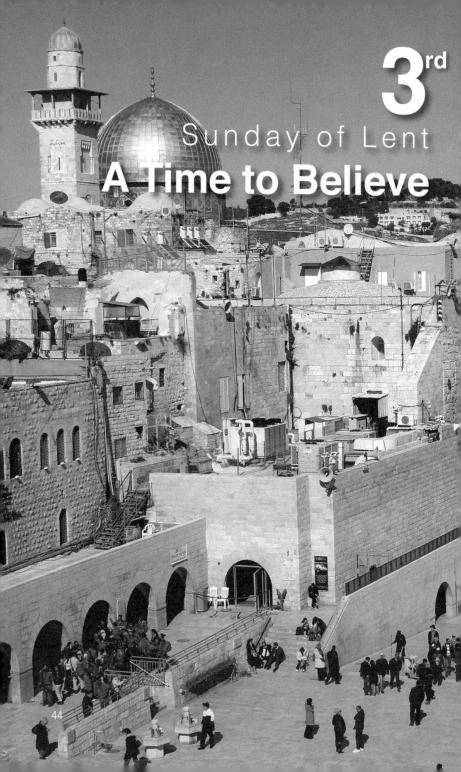

3**rd**
Sunday of Lent
**A Time to Believe**

44

"Zeal for thy house will consume me."

—John 2:17

Ask someone to pray in their own words, or read aloud the prayer below slowly as others pray along silently.

**Prayer for Guidance by St. Thomas Aquinas**

**In the name of the Father, and of the Son, and of the Holy Spirit.**

Creator past all telling,
you have appointed from the treasures
of your wisdom
the hierarchies of angels,
disposing them in wondrous order
above the bright heavens,
and have so beautifully set out all parts of the
universe.

You we call the true fount of wisdom
and the noble origin of all things.
Be pleased to shed
on the darkness of mind in which I was born,
the twofold beam of your light
and warmth to dispel my ignorance and sin.
You make eloquent the tongues of children.
Then instruct my speech
and touch my lips with graciousness.
Make me keen to understand, quick to learn,
able to remember;
make me delicate to interpret and ready to speak.
Guide my going in and going forward,
and lead home my going forth.
You are true God and true man,
and live for ever and ever.[1]

**Amen.**

---

[1] "Prayer Before Study," CatholiCity, accessed on March 10, 2017, http://www.catholicity.com/prayer/prayer-before-study.html.

1. Did anyone pray with the second reading from Romans before Sunday Mass, or the reading from Fr. Thomas Keating? How was that for you?

2. What is "righteous anger"? How would you describe it? Have you ever experienced it?

Ask two people to read this explanation aloud:

Before the Romans destroyed the second temple in 70 AD, Jews visited Jerusalem throughout the year, observing religious holidays with animal sacrifices at the Temple. The Temple building and precinct were massive, covering one-sixth of the land area in Jerusalem.[1]

The Court of the Gentiles where this Gospel story takes place was part of the Temple complex. It contained a large open outdoor area, very crowded with pilgrims, the animals sacrificed for Passover, and priests and Levites directing activity. Traders sold cattle, sheep, or goats to rich Jews; poorer Jews brought their own animals or bought pigeons. The money

[1] This painting conveys the enormity of the Temple during Jesus' time. Search "Brooklyn Museum Jerusalem Temple," or use this URL: https://en.wikipedia.org/wiki/Second_Temple#/media/File:Brooklyn_Museum_-_Reconstruction_of_Jerusalem_and_the_Temple_of_Herod_(R%C3%A9constitution_de_J%C3%A9rusalem_et_du_temple_d%27H%C3%A9rode)_-_James_Tissot.jpg.

changers made it possible for Jews to pay the Temple tax since Jews from other lands brought foreign currency. At Passover, the most important Jewish holiday of the year, large numbers of people would have been in the Temple precincts, including Gentile worshippers who were not allowed into the sanctuary.

Ask one person to read the Scripture passage aloud.

# John 2:13-25

[13] The Passover of the Jews was at hand, and Jesus went up to Jerusalem. [14] In the temple he found those who were selling oxen and sheep and pigeons, and the money-changers at their business. [15] And making a whip of cords, he drove them all, with the sheep and oxen, out of the temple; and he poured out the coins of the money-changers and overturned their tables. [16] And he told those who sold the pigeons, "Take these things away; you shall not make my Father's house a house of trade." [17] His disciples remembered that it was written, "Zeal for thy house will consume me." [18] The Jews then said to him, "What sign have you to show us for doing this?" [19] Jesus answered them, "Destroy this temple, and in three days I will raise it up." [20] The Jews then said, "It has taken forty-six years to build this temple, and will you raise it up in three days?" [21] But he spoke of the temple of his body. [22] When therefore he was raised from the dead, his disciples remembered that he had said this; and they believed the scripture and the word which Jesus had spoken.

[23] Now when he was in Jerusalem at the Passover feast, many believed in his name when they saw the signs which

he did; <sup>24</sup> but Jesus did not trust himself to them, <sup>25</sup> because he knew all men and needed no one to bear witness of man; for he himself knew what was in man.

1. What did Jesus do? List and describe his actions. If any-one has seen animals herded, please share what that may have looked like in the Temple courtyard.

2. How is the scene transformed when Jesus begins to act? In what ways might the different types of people present in the courtyard have reacted?

3. What Scripture passage comes to the disciples' minds as they observe Jesus' action (verse 17), and what does that tell us about Jesus' attitude and tone?

4. Would you say you have ever felt "zeal" for God's house, or for Jesus? If yes, what were the circumstances? If not, what do you think it would take for you to feel zealous for God?

5. Jesus equates his body with the Temple in verses 19-21. What are some of the implications of this statement? What does it mean for his followers?

6. Why do you think "the Jews" asked for a sign (verse 18)? What do you think they were hoping Jesus would do?

7. Could there be a good reason to ask God for a sign? What would be a good motivation?

8. Have you ever asked God for a sign? Would anyone be willing to share about that? What was it that you wanted? Did you feel that you received what you'd hoped for, or something else, or nothing?

Ask one person to read the Scripture passage aloud.

# 1 Corinthians 1:22-25

[22] For Jews demand signs and Greeks seek wisdom, [23] but we preach Christ crucified, a stumbling block to Jews and folly to Gentiles, [24] but to those who are called, both Jews and Greeks, Christ the power of God and the wisdom of God. [25] For the foolishness of God is wiser than men, and the weakness of God is stronger than men.

9. Has the cross ever been a "stumbling block" for you? Would someone be willing to share about that?

10. Would you say you are more inclined to seek signs from God, or pursue intellectual ideas about God (wisdom), or some combination of both? Maybe you tend to want something else altogether from God? **If so,** what is that?

11. Whatever you tend to seek from God, how would you say that tendency affects your spiritual life and our group interactions?

12. How do you experience Christ as "the power of God and the wisdom of God" in your life (verse 24)? Or would you say that these are ideas that you believe but don't necessarily experience?

13. How could people who don't feel they experience the power and wisdom of God seek it?

Commit to praying for fifteen minutes on three days this week. That's just 1% of your day and 3% of your whole week!

On one day, pray with the first reading for this Sunday that we didn't have time to discuss: Exodus 20:1-17, the Ten Commandments. The commandments can help us to see where and how God is calling us to live our beliefs more fully, or to act more lovingly or with more integrity. Read over them prayerfully, and then ask Jesus about which commandments you could observe better or more wholeheartedly. Ask the Holy Spirit to remind you of specific commandments within your day when you need a reminder. If you struggle with even wanting to change a behavior, ask the Father for the grace to *desire* to observe a commandment more fully and faithfully. On other days, either pray with the daily Mass readings on the opposite page using the instructions in Appendix B for *lectio divina*, or choose from these suggestions:

- If your belief in the power of the cross feels tepid or uncertain, talk to someone with strong belief this week. Express your own doubts and uncertainty, and ask how that person came to such a firm belief.

- In Catholic tradition, observing Lent includes giving alms. If you haven't given to the poor as part of your Lenten sacrifice, ask Jesus to move your heart with compassion toward the person or organization he wants you to support. If nothing comes to mind, find out how to help in a food pantry or a meal program. Give a gift to Catholic Relief Services, Catholic Charities, or any service organization. If you feel led to give monetarily, go out of your way to give your contribution in secret. Jesus promises that the Father rewards those who give in secret (Matthew 6:1-4).

• If you haven't planned to fast or practice other penances this Lent, think of something you could do this week out of love for Jesus. Perhaps you might skip a meal to spend time with a co-worker who seems lonely. Maybe you could visit an elderly family member you rarely see because you don't enjoy being there. Through our penances and acts of service, we concretely choose to love God and others above ourselves.

## This Week's Mass Readings:
Monday: 2 Kgs 5:1-15a • Ps 42:2-3; 43:3-4 • Lk 4:24-30
Tuesday: Dn 3:25, 34-43 • Ps 25:4-9 • Mt 18:21-35
Wednesday: Dt 4:1, 5-9 • Ps 147:12-13, 15-16, 19-20 • Mt 5:17-19
Thursday: Jer 7:23-28 • Ps 95:1-2, 6-9 • Lk 11:14-23
Friday: Hos 14:2-10 • Ps 81:6-11, 14, 17 • Mk 12:28-34
Saturday: Hos 6:1-6 • Ps 51:3-4, 18-21 • Lk 18:9-14

Instead of asking for petitions that one person summarizes in a prayer, this week, after praying the Sign of the Cross, each person should take turns asking God directly for whatever he or she needs. Jesus told us to ask, knock, and seek (Matthew 7:7): we should feel free to do that even for our own needs and even in front of others in a group. Familiar prayers we all know and can say together have their place, but a new depth comes to group prayer when each of us starts to express our own needs or our gratitude to God directly. After people have prayed, the person who opens the prayer should close with the Glory Be.

# 4<sup>th</sup>

Sunday of Lent

## A Time to Choose the Light

The light has come into the world, and people loved darkness rather than light.

—John 3:19 (NRSV)

Ask someone to read the following
 paragraph:

We will pray the following psalm at Mass next Sunday.
It describes the grief of Jewish Temple musicians in
exile after they were deported to Babylon. The Babylo-
nians besieged Jerusalem, razed the Temple, and took
the religious and political leaders back home with them,
a common practice to prevent conquered peoples from
rising up again. Jerusalem remained in ruins with a
decimated population struggling to survive; Babylon
gained a highly educated, musically gifted, and admin-
istratively able group of slaves, including the prophet
Daniel, the subject of one Old Testament book.

Ask someone to pray in their own words
for the meeting before the group leader
begins the psalm. The group should
respond where it says, "All."

# Psalm 137

**In the name of the Father, and of the Son
and of the Holy Spirit.**

## Leader

By the waters of Babylon, there we sat down and wept, when we remembered Zion. On the willows there we hung up our lyres.

## All

If I forget you, O Jerusalem, let my right hand wither!

## Leader

For there our captors required of us songs, and our tormentors, mirth, saying, "Sing us one of the songs of Zion!"

## All

If I forget you, O Jerusalem, let my right hand wither!

## Leader

How shall we sing the LORD's song in a foreign land?

## All

If I forget you, O Jerusalem, let my right hand wither!

## Leader

If I forget you, O Jerusalem, let my right hand wither! Let my tongue cleave to the roof of my mouth, if I do not remember you, if I do not set Jerusalem above my highest joy!

## All

If I forget you, O Jerusalem, let my right hand wither!

## Amen.

1. Has anyone tried praying for fifteen minutes one day using the Scriptures? How did that go for you?

2. What is feeling exiled like? What has caused that feeling for you, or for someone you know?

Ask one person to read the Scripture passage aloud.

# 2 Chronicles 36:14-16,19-23

[14] All the leading priests and the people likewise were exceedingly unfaithful, following all the abominations of the nations; and they polluted the house of the LORD which he had hallowed in Jerusalem.

[15] The LORD, the God of their fathers, sent persistently to them by his messengers, because he had compassion on his people and on his dwelling place; [16] but they kept mocking the messengers of God, despising his words, and scoffing at his prophets, till the wrath of the LORD rose against his people, till there was no remedy. . . .

[19] And they [the Chaldeans, v. 17, another term for Babylonians] burned the house of God, and broke down the wall of Jerusalem, and burned all its palaces with fire, and destroyed all its precious vessels. [20] He [the King of the Chaldeans] took into exile in Babylon

those who had escaped from the sword, and they became servants to him and to his sons until the establishment of the kingdom of Persia, [21] to fulfil the word of the LORD by the mouth of Jeremiah, until the land had enjoyed its sabbaths. All the days that it lay desolate it kept sabbath, to fulfil seventy years.

[22] Now in the first year of Cyrus king of Persia, that the word of the LORD by the mouth of Jeremiah might be accomplished, the LORD stirred up the spirit of Cyrus king of Persia so that he made a proclamation throughout all his kingdom and also put it in writing: [23] "Thus says Cyrus king of Persia, 'The LORD, the God of heaven, has given me all the kingdoms of the earth, and he has charged me to build him a house at Jerusalem, which is in Judah. Whoever is among you of all his people, may the LORD his God be with him. Let him go up.'"

1. How does the Book of Chronicles explain why Jerusalem fell to Babylon (verses 14-16)?

2. The Church understands the Babylonian exile as a period of purification.[1] How do you think exile purifies people? What happens in people's exterior and interior lives in exile that brings about a kind of "cleansing"?

---

[1] *Catechism of the Catholic Church*, 710 : "The forgetting of the Law and the infidelity to the covenant end in death: it is the Exile, apparently the failure of the promises, which is in fact the mysterious fidelity of the Savior God and the beginning of a promised restoration, but according to the Spirit. The People of God had to suffer this purification. In God's plan, the Exile already stands in the shadow of the Cross, and the Remnant of the poor that returns from the Exile is one of the most transparent prefigurations of the Church."

Ask one person to read the Scripture passage aloud.

# John 3:14-21

[14] "And as Moses lifted up the serpent in the wilderness, so must the Son of man be lifted up, [15] that whoever believes in him may have eternal life."

[16] For God so loved the world that he gave his only Son, that whoever believes in him should not perish but have eternal life. [17] For God sent the Son into the world, not to condemn the world, but that the world might be saved through him. [18] He who believes in him is not condemned; he who does not believe is condemned already, because he has not believed in the name of the only Son of God. [19] And this is the judgment, that the light has come into the world, and men loved darkness rather than light, because their deeds were evil. [20] For every one who does evil hates the light, and does not come to the light, lest his deeds should be exposed. [21] But he who does what is true comes to the light, that it may be clearly seen that his deeds have been wrought in God.

3. In verses 16-17, St. John explains why God sent Jesus into the world. Would anyone be willing to share how your experiences clearly reflect, or fail to reflect, this understanding of why Jesus came?

4. Let's toss out some words that we associate with physical light. (*Allow 30 seconds to a minute.*) Now let's do the same with physical darkness. (*Allow 30 seconds to a minute.*) How does naming these add to your understanding of what Jesus' presence in the world means?

5. What evidence from Jesus' life demonstrates that "the light has come into the world" (verse 19) but that people preferred the darkness?

6. How is the darkness that St. John describes like exile, and how is it different?

7. Why do you think we sometimes prefer the "darkness" or being "exiled" —isolated and alienated—more than life-giving community, connection with other Christians, and committed relationships?

8. How does John 3:20 explain the human tendency to love darkness? Conversely, how does John 3:21 explain the motivation for moving toward Jesus? Do the reasons seem accurate to you? Why or why not?

9. If you've experienced a time when you have been motivated to move out of the darkness into the light, would you be able to explain what made you recognize the "darkness" as darkness, the "exile" as exile? Would anyone be willing to share about this?

10. Has anyone had an experience in which the Holy Spirit moved you out of the darkness when you had been unable to do so under your own power, or have you witnessed this in someone else? Would you be willing to share about how you or someone else came to love the light?

Commit to praying for fifteen minutes a day on four days this week.

## Day 1

Use Appendix B to pray for at least fifteen minutes with the Gospel reading for this coming Sunday, John 3:14-21. It's worth revisiting this Scripture passage on our own. We rarely talk openly about the darkness in our lives for obvious reasons: we hide in the darkness what we're ashamed to bring into the light.

During your prayer, talk to Jesus about what you hide. Ask him to help you love him more than the protection of the darkness. Ask for the trust you need to believe that what God has for you in the light will make you far happier than anything else ever could. If God tells you to do anything about this area of struggle, do it immediately, or as soon as possible.

One of the best ways to open our darkness to the light of the world is to share the shadowy areas of our lives with someone else. The Sacrament of Reconciliation provides a safe way to do that. If you're Catholic and you have not already been to Confession this Lent, God longs to help you love the light, his son, Jesus! Nothing has the power to transform pain and shame into abundant life as the presence of Jesus with us in Confession through the priest, acting *in persona Christi*.[1]

---

[1] This is Latin for "in the person of Christ."

If you're squirming right now, you're not alone. It's natural to feel embarrassment or discomfort about Confession. Sin isn't pretty. Something is wrong with us if we don't feel bad when we hurt others, and hurting ourselves packs its own lasting punch, whether we feel guilty or not. Even simply thinking that we haven't done the good God wants us to do leaves us feeling empty and purposeless.

When fear or pride keeps us from Confession, we try to forget our failures and move on. But the effects of sin don't—they remain, hurting us. That's why the Church understands Reconciliation as a healing sacrament. God made us to be in relationships, not alone in our private darkness. He wired us that way. Sin short-circuits the wiring. The grace of Reconciliation powerfully repairs our connection to God and the people in our lives.

You might think, "I don't need to talk to a priest. I talk to God about my sins." Pope Francis says that's like confessing through e-mail!

Some say: "Ah, I confess to God." But . . . it's like confessing by e-mail, no? God is far away, I say things, and there's no face-to-face, no eye-to-eye contact. Paul confesses his weakness to the brethren face-to-face.[2]

Jesus knew how important face-to-face encounter is. Freedom from the darkness doesn't come to us in isolation or exile. Human contact brings us back into human community. It's our way home as surely as the road from Babylon led the deported Jews back to Jerusalem. Jesus made this road when he gave the apostles the power to free people: "Whatever you loose on earth shall be loosed

[2] "Pope Francis: Confess Sins with Concreteness and Sincerity," Vatican Radio, October 25, 2013, http://www.news.va/en/news/pope-francis-confess-sins-with-concreteness-and-si.

in heaven" (Matthew 16:19). Going to Confession brings us back into communion and guarantees access to that power.

Don't let embarrassment keep you from the healing and consolation that God wants to give you. Appendix D provides a guide to the Sacrament of Reconciliation. If that isn't sufficient to relieve your fears, talk to someone you know who participates in the sacrament and ask them about their experience. Even better, ask if they would accompany you to church when you go to Confession.

If you're not Catholic, the priest is available to you as he is for Catholics. It's very comforting to share the weight of our burdens with another, especially with clergy who are trained and experienced in helping people walk with the Lord.

No matter whether you are a believer, non-believer, Catholic, or other Christian, God loves you and wants you to be with him. "A broken and contrite heart, O God, thou wilt not despise" (Psalm 51:17). Often it's when we're most hurting that we open up to the healing the Lord wants to pour into our hearts, and to the only relationship that saves us (John 3:17).

## Day 2

Pray with the second reading below before Sunday using the questions that follow.

# Ephesians 2:4-10

[4] But God, who is rich in mercy, out of the great love with which he loved us, [5] even when we were dead through our trespasses, made us alive together with Christ (by grace you have been saved), [6] and raised us up with him, and made us sit with him in the heavenly places in Christ Jesus, [7] that in the coming ages he might show the

immeasurable riches of his grace in kindness toward us in Christ Jesus. [8] For by grace you have been saved through faith; and this is not your own doing, it is the gift of God— [9] not because of works, lest any man should boast. [10] For we are his workmanship, created in Christ Jesus for good works, which God prepared beforehand, that we should walk in them.

1. How does St. Paul explain why God sent Jesus, his Son (verses 4-7)? How does he explain it differently than St. John did in John 3:16-17?

2. If you've been baptized, would you say that you've experienced the reality that you have been saved by grace in that sacrament? How could you seek to experience this truth if you haven't?

3. Do you feel that God shows the riches of his grace in kindness toward you, and that happens somehow "in Christ Jesus" (verse 7)? If not, ask God right now to show you his love in your life, how it has been there in the past, and the ways he is pouring out his love in your life right now. If so, remember times when you've felt sure of the "riches of his grace" and thank God for it.

4. What do you feel would be an appropriate response in your life to the kindness and love that God has shown you? Talk to Jesus about it.

## Day 3

For a prayer specifically designed to help us choose light over darkness, see Appendix C. It provides a modified version of an extended meditation from the *Spiritual Exercises* by St. Ignatius of Loyola, the founder of the Jesuit order. "The Two Standards" refers to banners, or flags, on a field of battle that troops rallied around during warfare. (Ignatius was a military man before his conversion; he drew on those experiences for metaphors that could help others grow spiritually.) In "The Two Standards," he asks us to imagine opposing forces of good and evil as armies facing off, each gathered under its own standard.

## Other Days

Don't let the fact that there are only three days of prayer suggestions here keep you from praying the other days this week! We recommend a specific number of days to encourage you beyond whatever you usually do. If you already pray daily, keep doing it. On some days, use our suggestions to expand the ways you communicate with God. Think of these as different kinds of activities with God. If you bowled with someone once a week, that relationship would grow if you also decided to meet for coffee and conversation on another day. Similarly with prayer: praying with Scripture allows God to speak to us in different ways than other prayer methods. It will help you get to know Jesus better and deepen your relationship with him.

The daily Mass readings provide an excellent resource for prayer that fits with the liturgical season. To make reading these Scripture passages more prayerful and enriching, use Appendix B, especially the brief instructions on *lectio divina*, an ancient way to pray with the Scriptures.

## This Week's Mass Readings:

Monday: Is 65:17-21 • Ps 30:2, 4-6, 11-13 • Jn 4:43-54

Tuesday: Ez 47:1-9, 12 • Ps 46:2-3, 5-6, 8-9 • Jn 5:1-16

Wednesday: Is 49:8-15 • Ps 145:8-9, 13-14, 17-18 • Jn 5:17-30

Thursday: Ex 32:7-14 • Ps 106:19-23 • Jn 5:31-47

Friday: Wis 2:1a, 12-22 • Ps 34:17-21, 23 • Jn 7:1-2, 10, 25-30

Saturday: Jer 11:18-20 • Ps 7:2-3, 9-12 • Jn 7:40-53

Make the Sign of the Cross, and then again voice your prayer needs directly to God. After everyone has had a chance to ask God for what they need, pray together the Prayer of St. Francis on the opposite page.

**In the name of the Father, and of the Son and of the Holy Spirit.**

*(Individual petitions)*

# All

Lord, make me an instrument of your peace
where there is hatred, let me sow love;
where there is injury, pardon;
where there is doubt, faith;
where there is despair, hope;
where there is darkness, light;
where there is sadness, joy.

O divine Master, grant that I may not so much seek
to be consoled as to console,
to be understood as to understand,
to be loved as to love.
For it is in giving that we receive,
it is in pardoning that we are pardoned,
and it is in dying that we are born to eternal life.[1]

# Amen.

---

[1] "Peace Prayer of Saint Francis," Loyola Press, http://www.loyolapress.com/our-catholic-faith/prayer/traditional-catholic-prayers/saints-prayers/peace-prayer-of-saint-francis.

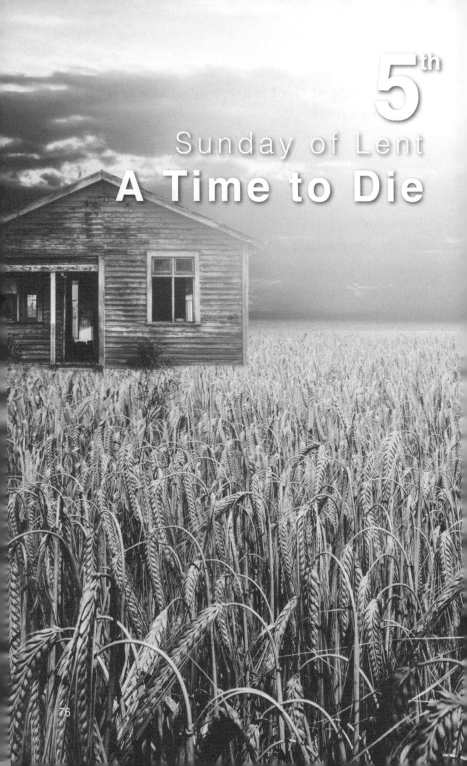

# 5th
## Sunday of Lent
# A Time to Die

"Unless a grain of wheat falls into the earth and dies, it remains alone; but if it dies, it bears much fruit."
—John 12:24

Ask someone to pray in their own words, and then read aloud the following prayer slowly as others pray along silently.

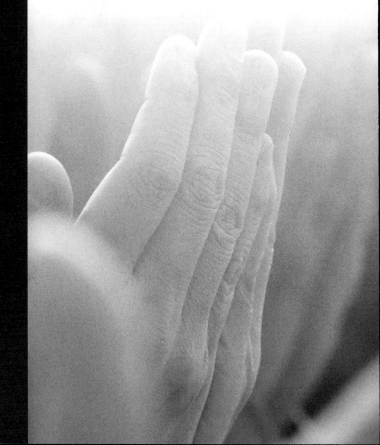

**In the name of the Father, and of the Son, and of the Holy Spirit.**

God our Father, we believe that you are here with us.
We gather as your sons and daughters,
drawn by your Son and enlightened by the Holy Spirit.

Jesus, through our time together,
help us to hear your invitation to follow you more
courageously.

Holy Spirit, open our hearts to the Scriptures,
that through our meditation,
we might desire to give ourselves
more fully and generously
as Jesus did to our Father.

We pray this through Christ our Lord.

**Amen.**

1. Did anyone pray with the Ignatius meditation on the Two Standards? How did that go?

2. What is most frightening to you about dying?

Ask one person to read the Scripture passage aloud.

# Hebrews 5:7-9

[7] In the days of his flesh, Jesus offered up prayers and supplications, with loud cries and tears, to him who was able to save him from death, and he was heard for his godly fear. [8] Although he was a Son, he learned obedience through what he suffered; [9] and being made perfect he became the source of eternal salvation to all who obey him.

Ask one person to read the Scripture passage aloud.

# John 12:20-33

[20] Now among those who went up to worship at the feast were some Greeks. [21] So these came to Philip, who was from Beth-sa´ida in Galilee, and said to him, "Sir, we wish to see Jesus." [22] Philip went and told Andrew; Andrew went with Philip and they told Jesus. [23] And Jesus answered them, "The hour has come for the Son

of man to be glorified. [24] Truly, truly, I say to you, unless a grain of wheat falls into the earth and dies, it remains alone; but if it dies, it bears much fruit. [25] He who loves his life loses it, and he who hates his life in this world will keep it for eternal life. [26] If any one serves me, he must follow me; and where I am, there shall my servant be also; if any one serves me, the Father will honor him.

[27] "Now is my soul troubled. And what shall I say? 'Father, save me from this hour'? No, for this purpose I have come to this hour. [28] Father, glorify thy name." Then a voice came from heaven, "I have glorified it, and I will glorify it again." [29] The crowd standing by heard it and said that it had thundered. Others said, "An angel has spoken to him." [30] Jesus answered, "This voice has come for your sake, not for mine. [31] Now is the judgment of this world, now shall the ruler of this world be cast out; [32] and I, when I am lifted up from the earth, will draw all men to myself." [33] He said this to show by what death he was to die.

1. Did anything catch your attention in these readings?

2. What Lenten themes did you observe?

3. Would someone please describe the sequence of events that led up to Jesus' speech? (Pause.) Why do you think St. John provided so much detail?

4. Why might Greeks (non-Jews) have been seeking Jesus?

5. How would you describe Jesus' tone and mood in the Gospel passage, and why do you think he would have spoken in this way?

6. How does the reading from John relate to the verses describing Jesus from the Letter to the Hebrews?

7. Do you think it applied just to him or to others as well when Jesus said that if a seed dies, it bears much fruit, and if you hate your life in this world, you keep it for eternal life? Please explain your reasons.

8. Do you think this frightened the disciples? Should it have frightened them?

9. Looking to the Gospel and the Letter to the Hebrews, how did Jesus battle the temptation to fear?

10. Has anyone ever experienced the need to put something "old" to death—perhaps a sin pattern, a habit, or a way of thinking—in order for rebirth and renewal to happen in your life? *(Pause.)* Would someone be willing to share about this?

11. We believe that Jesus sympathizes with our weaknesses and was tempted in every way that we are, yet did not sin (Hebrews 4:15). What practical steps could we take that would help us cling to Jesus more confidently through our daily weaknesses and our times of "loud cries and tears" (5:7)?

12. Has anything ever helped you to trust God more, or helped you hand over the reins of your life to God more willingly?

13. Is there any area of your life where the Holy Spirit might be giving you a glimpse of new life that could come from letting go of something you've felt attached to or controlled by? Would someone be willing to share about that?

It's the last week of Lent. Holy Week begins in the sixth week with Palm Sunday. End your Lent on a high note by praying fifteen minutes every day this week. You will never know what God can do in your life through daily prayer unless you pray daily! If you pray every day for a week, you will have given God just 7% of your time over seven days. If God is who we say he is, that's not much time to devote to the One who made you and all of creation!

Praying with the daily Mass readings not only easily fills that fifteen minutes, but the Scripture passages lead thematically to Holy Week, deepening your experience of Jesus' death and resurrection. Revisit Appendix B if you need a reminder about how to do *lectio divina*.

If you haven't yet made a Lenten confession, plan a time to do it this week. A guide to the Sacrament of Reconciliation appears in Appendix D. If the sacrament still seems too difficult, and you haven't yet reached out to someone who participates in this sacrament, commit to doing that this week. Be sure to ask that person why they go to Confession and what it does for them.

Here are some other ideas for prayer if you need them:

- Take some time every day this week to ask yourself: what do I cling to in place of Christ? This could take many different forms— food, a relationship, a false image of yourself that you project to the world, your own abilities, or a habit of worry. The Lord is indeed the light of the world, but he isn't the kind of God who will force his light into your life. He always entices. We respond by entering into or deepening our relationship with him. Relationships take time. Is there something in your life you want to change to make room for God? Pray about that this week.

Lift up to Jesus anything you are clinging to as a substitute for what can really satisfy you—Jesus and a relationship with him. You can do this with words or visually. Say something such as this in your own words: "Lord, this is something that keeps me from you, from peace, from living the life of peace you meant for me to live. Help me give this to you, Lord. Please take it from me. I know it is not within my power to 'fix' myself. Only your love can change this. I surrender it to you, O Lord."

Or if words feel awkward or unnatural, visualize giving yourself to Christ. Imagine him on the other side of a door. Stand on your side of the door, clinging to the thing that keeps you from opening it. Think of the ways you rely on this prop. Does it really accomplish what you want it to accomplish? Does it keep you safe, make you happy, prevent disaster, make you lovable? Try to identify all the hopes that you have placed in this behavior, state of mind, or psychological propensity. When you can see that it has actually given you none of the things you really want, then you will be ready to open the door. Give that thing to which you cling to Jesus, who is standing on the other side. He is waiting to give you what you really need; he can break the power it has had in your life.

- Consider these questions in prayer this week, remembering that Jesus said he would draw all men and women to himself when he was lifted up: What holds me back from Christ? Am I stopping myself from being drawn to him? Do I

  - fear he will take something away from me?
  - find it hard to believe he really is trying to draw me to himself?
  - believe lies that "the ruler of this world" tells me to keep me away from Christ (John 12:31)?
  - doubt that being drawn to him would be the greatest thing that could happen in my life?

## This Week's Mass Readings:

Monday: Dn 13:1-9, 15-17, 19-30, 33-62 • Ps 23:1-6 • Jn 8:1-11
Tuesday: Nm 21:4-9 • Ps 102:2-3, 16-21 • Jn 8:21-30
Wednesday: Dn 3:14-20, 91-92, 95 • Dn 3:52-56 • Jn 8:31-42
Thursday: Gn 17:3-9 • Ps 105:4-9 • Jn 8:51-59
Friday: Jer 20:10-13 • Ps 18:2-7 • Jn 10:31-42
Saturday: Ez 37:21-28 • Jer 31:10-13 • Jn 11:45-56

Use the instructions from the first week's closing prayer to pray for each other. After the group prays for one another together, ask someone to read aloud the following prayer slowly as others pray along silently.

**In the name of the Father, and of the Son, and of the Holy Spirit.**

Lord, we want to give ourselves more fully to you.
You know that our faith is too small,
our vision skewed,
our fears great.
Grant us a supernatural outlook
so that we might see the grain of wheat
in our lives
and want what you want.
Please make us more sensitive to
the ways your Holy Spirit draws us to yourself.
We do not want to miss your invitations.
Please help us to be faithful to your promptings.
We pray for the courage to be molded anew
and the trust to believe the promise of your glory.
We pray this through Christ our Lord.

**Amen.**

# Palm Sunday of the Lord's Passion
# A Time to Weep

I gave my back to those
who struck me.

—Isaiah 50:6 (NRSV)

Ask someone to pray in their own words,
or read aloud the following prayer slowly as
others pray along silently.

**In the name of the Father, and of the Son, and of
the Holy Spirit.**

Behold me, my beloved Jesus,
weighed down under the burden of my trials
and sufferings;
 I cast myself at your feet,
 that you may renew my strength and my courage,
 while I rest here in your presence.
Permit me to lay down my cross in your Sacred Heart,
 for only your infinite goodness can sustain me;
 only your love can help me bear my cross;
 only your powerful hand can lighten its weight.
O Divine King, Jesus,
 whose heart is so compassionate to the afflicted,
 I wish to live in you;
 suffer and die in you.
During my life be to me my model and my support;
 At the hour of my death,
be my hope and my refuge.[1]

**Amen.**

[1] "Prayer in Time of Suffering," Catholic Online Prayers website, http://www.
catholic.org/prayers/prayer.php?p=873.

1. Have you ever had a time when the events around Jesus' death related to your life in a particularly powerful way? Some incidents include Peter denying Jesus, Judas betraying Jesus, enemies speaking against Jesus during his trial, cruel men taunting and torturing Jesus, Jesus feeling abandoned by the disciples, and Jesus feeling forsaken by God.

The citation for the full Gospel reading appears on the opposite page, but we include only the sections of the text covered in questions. This will allow for prayer and consideration over significant moments.

Ask one person to read the Scripture passage aloud.

# Mark 14:17–15:47

14:17 And when it was evening he came with the twelve. 18 And as they were at table eating, Jesus said, "Truly, I say to you, one of you will betray me, one who is eating with me." 19 They began to be sorrowful, and to say to him one after another, "Is it I?" 20 He said to them, "It is one of the twelve, one who is dipping bread in the same dish with me. 21 For the Son of man goes as it is written of him, but woe to that man by whom the Son of man is betrayed! It would have been better for that man if he had not been born."

22 And as they were eating, he took bread, and blessed, and broke it, and gave it to them, and said, "Take; this is my body." 23 And he took a cup, and when he had given thanks he gave it to them, and they all drank of it. 24 And he said to them, "This is my blood of the covenant, which is poured out for many. 25 Truly, I say to you, I shall not drink again of the fruit of the vine until that day when I drink it new in the kingdom of God."

26 And when they had sung a hymn, they went out to the Mount of Olives. 27 And Jesus said to them, "You will all fall away; for it is written, 'I will strike the shepherd, and the sheep will be scattered.' 28 But after I am raised up, I will go before you to Galilee." 29 Peter said to him, "Even though they all fall away, I will not." 30 And Jesus said to him, "Truly, I say to you, this very night, before the cock crows twice, you will deny me three times." 31 But he said vehemently, "If I must die with you, I will not deny you." And they all said the same.

1. Why do you think Jesus told his disciples that one of them would betray him? Since it seemed to be inevitable, what would have made Jesus say this? Consider the effect his words have on his followers in your answer (verse 19).

2. Here is the first celebration of the Lord's Supper and the institution of the Eucharist. What do you think the disciples thought when Jesus was blessing and sharing the meal with these words?

3. After Jesus declared that one of them would betray him, and after saying such ominous words over their meal, what do you think the tone of the group would have been when they went to the Mount of Olives? How might Jesus' words there have further influenced the tone?

4. How would you describe Peter's declaration that he will not deny Jesus (verse 29)? What could have motivated such a comment?

Ask one person to read the Scripture passage aloud.

14:32 And they went to a place which was called Gethsem´ane; and he said to his disciples, "Sit here, while I pray." 33 And he took with him Peter and James and John, and began to be greatly distressed and troubled. 34 And he said to them, "My soul is very sorrowful, even to death; remain here, and watch." 35 And going a little farther, he fell on the ground and prayed that, if it were possible, the hour might pass from him. 36 And he said, "Abba, Father, all things are possible to thee; remove this cup from me; yet not what I will, but what thou wilt." 37 And he came and found them sleeping, and he said to Peter, "Simon, are you asleep? Could you not watch one hour? 38 Watch and pray that you may not enter into temptation; the spirit indeed is willing, but the flesh is weak." 39 And again he went away and prayed, saying the same words. 40 And again he came and found them sleeping, for their eyes were very heavy; and they did not know what to answer him. 41 And he came the third time, and said to them, "Are you still sleeping and taking your rest? It is enough; the hour has come; the Son of man is betrayed into the hands of sinners. 42 Rise, let us be going; see, my betrayer is at hand."

5. What effect might Jesus' statement about his sorrow in verse 34 have had on Peter, James, and John?

6. Jesus falls on the ground when he begins to pray. What does that indicate about his state of mind and the prayer he prays?

7. Would anyone be willing to share about a time that you prayed in extreme sorrow or distress? What did your prayer sound like? How does this inform your understanding of Jesus' prayer at Gethsemane?

8. How do you think the disciples would have felt looking back on their last hour with Jesus at Gethsemane?

9. Have you ever felt that you failed someone who was in deep sorrow? If you would be willing to share about that, how did you deal with that feeling afterward?

## Ask one person to read the Scripture passage aloud.

[14:43] And immediately, while he was still speaking, Judas came, one of the twelve, and with him a crowd with swords and clubs, from the chief priests and the scribes and the elders. [44] Now the betrayer had given them a sign, saying, "The one I shall kiss is the man; seize him and lead him away safely." [45] And when he came, he went up to him at once, and said, "Master!" And he kissed him. [46] And they laid hands on him and seized him. [47] But one of those who stood by drew his sword, and struck the slave of the high priest and cut off his ear. [48] And Jesus said to them, "Have you come out as against a robber, with swords and clubs to capture me? [49] Day after day I was with you in the temple teaching, and you did not seize me. But let the scriptures be fulfilled." [50] And they all forsook him, and fled.

[51] And a young man followed him, with nothing but a linen cloth about his body; and they seized him, [52] but he left the linen cloth and ran away naked.

10. Christian tradition has held that the young man who ran off in only the linen cloth was Mark himself, the Gospel writer. (This detail appears in no other Gospel account.) How does that change your understanding of why this is included in the story? If it was Mark, how do you think he felt about what he did?

Ask one person to read the Scripture passage aloud.

[14:60] And the high priest stood up in the midst, and asked Jesus, "Have you no answer to make? What is it that these men testify against you?" [61] But he was silent and made no answer. Again the high priest asked him, "Are you the Christ, the Son of the Blessed?" [62] And Jesus said, "I am; and you will see the Son of man sitting at the right hand of Power, and coming with the clouds of heaven." [63] And the high priest tore his mantle, and said, "Why do we still need witnesses? [64] You have heard his blasphemy. What is your decision?" And they all condemned him as deserving death. [65] And some began to spit on him, and to cover his face, and to strike him, saying to him, "Prophesy!" And the guards received him with blows.

11. What emotions might have been behind Caiaphas' determination that Jesus should die? How would you explain the viciousness of the attacks on Jesus after he speaks?

Ask one person to read the Scripture passage aloud. When you reach the moment at verse 37 when Jesus dies, please allow a minute of silence.

<sup>15:22</sup> And they brought him to the place called Gol'gotha (which means the place of a skull). <sup>23</sup> And they offered him wine mingled with myrrh; but he did not take it. <sup>24</sup> And they crucified him, and divided his garments among them, casting lots for them, to decide what each should take. <sup>25</sup> And it was the third hour, when they crucified him. <sup>26</sup> And the inscription of the charge against him read, "The King of the Jews." <sup>27</sup> And with him they crucified two robbers, one on his right and one on his left. <sup>29</sup> And those who passed by derided him, wagging their heads, and saying, "Aha! You who would destroy the temple and build it in three days, <sup>30</sup> save yourself, and come down from the cross!" <sup>31</sup> So also the chief priests mocked him to one another with the scribes, saying, "He saved others; he cannot save himself. <sup>32</sup> Let the Christ, the King of Israel, come down now from the cross, that we may see and believe." Those who were crucified with him also reviled him.

<sup>33</sup> And when the sixth hour had come, there was darkness over the whole land until the ninth hour. <sup>34</sup> And at the ninth hour Jesus cried with a loud voice, "*E'lo-i, E'lo-i, la'ma sabach-tha'ni?*" which means, "My God, my God, why hast thou forsaken me?" <sup>35</sup> And some of the bystanders hearing it said, "Behold, he is calling Eli'jah." <sup>36</sup> And one ran and, filling a sponge full of vinegar, put it on a reed and gave it to him to drink, saying, "Wait, let us see whether Eli'jah will come to take him down." <sup>37</sup> And Jesus uttered a loud cry, and breathed his last.

*(Silence.)*

[38] And the curtain of the temple was torn in two, from top to bottom. [39] And when the centurion, who stood facing him, saw that he thus breathed his last, he said, "Truly this man was the Son of God!"

[40] There were also women looking on from afar, among whom were Mary Mag´dalene, and Mary the mother of James the younger and of Joses, and Salo´me, [41] who, when he was in Galilee, followed him, and ministered to him; and also many other women who came up with him to Jerusalem.

[42] And when evening had come, since it was the day of Preparation, that is, the day before the sabbath, [43] Joseph of Arimathe´a, a respected member of the council, who was also himself looking for the kingdom of God, took courage and went to Pilate, and asked for the body of Jesus. [44] And Pilate wondered if he were already dead; and summoning the centurion, he asked him whether he was already dead. [45] And when he learned from the centurion that he was dead, he granted the body to Joseph. [46] And he bought a linen shroud, and taking him down, wrapped him in the linen shroud, and laid him in a tomb which had been hewn out of the rock; and he rolled a stone against the door of the tomb. [47] Mary Mag´dalene and Mary the mother of Joses saw where he was laid.

12. If during this reading you experienced anything you hadn't previously in regard to Jesus' death, would you be willing to share about it?

13. Only Mark's Gospel says that Joseph of Arimathea "took courage" (verse 43). Why would his actions have required courage?

14. St. Mark also says that Joseph was "also himself looking

for the kingdom of God" (verse 43). How do you recognize someone who is "looking for the kingdom of God"? What characterizes such a person?

15. Would you say that you are looking for the kingdom of God? If so, how would people know this is true of you? Are there some ways in which you could live and act differently that would show you seek God's kingdom?

Holy Week focuses our attention on Jesus' suffering for us and our failures in the face of his suffering, as well as all suffering.

Prepare for the Triduum by praying with the particularly rich Holy Week daily Mass readings each day using the *lectio divina* technique described in Appendix B. The full meaning of Easter will be more available to you from meditating on these Scripture passages. Seek what Jesus has to say to you about your failings and sorrows. Talk to Jesus as personally as you can during the "respond" time of *lectio divina*.

In addition to praying with the readings each day, attend the Triduum services. These three Christian high holy days begin on Holy Thursday and culminate on Easter. The beautiful liturgies of the Triduum have the power to bring us into the mystery of Christ's death and resurrection as nothing else.

Plan to begin with the Mass of the Lord's Supper on Holy Thursday night, when the Church marks the institution of the Eucharist by the washing of feet. After Mass, the priest removes the consecrated bread from the Church to a chapel of repose where we watch and pray with Jesus as in the Garden of Gethsemane. We leave the tabernacle in Church open—an empty space where Jesus should be—to experience our Lord's absence as his followers did after his arrest.

The empty tabernacle, however, symbolizes much more. Jesus emptied himself for us. Before Holy Thursday, meditate on the hymn from Philippians that we read at Passion Sunday Mass:

Christ . . . did not count equality with God a thing to be grasped:,but emptied himself, taking the form of a servant, being born in the likeness of men. And being found in human form he humbled himself and became obedient unto death, even death on a cross. (Philippians 2:5-8)

Consider the emptiness Christ knew standing before the courts, in the praetorium, carrying his cross, nailed to it on Golgotha. Empty yourself to share in his suffering. Clearing out our schedules can be a way to empty ourselves of our busyness, our self-importance, and our habitual activities that can distract us from God. Persevere even if you feel agitated by time that seems "wasted." Not infrequently, busy lives can hide the truth that boredom in prayer is the real reason we don't pray, not our many responsibilities and duties. Self-emptying demands putting aside what usually occupies our internal lives. Be prepared for that to be difficult, and trust that God will do something with this humbling experience!

At the Good Friday prayer service, we commemorate the day Jesus suffered and died by reading or singing the Passion according to John. We venerate the cross, the reminder of what Christ underwent for our salvation, and for Christians, the sign of God's power and wisdom (Week 3). It is the promise that life will triumph over suffering and death. At the end of the service, the priest brings the consecrated bread reserved after Holy Thursday's Mass from the chapel of repose to distribute before blessing and dispersing the congregation.

The Great Vigil on Saturday night officially includes seven readings from the Old Testament[2] and two from the New, as well as baptisms, confirmations, and first Eucharist for the neophytes.

---

[2] Sometimes pastors choose to proclaim fewer readings. Only three are mandatory.

It is a long service, but well worth it. Witnessing adult baptism can be an intense and powerful experience even if we don't know the person being baptized. If you can attend this service, do so!

On Good Friday, meditate for at least ten minutes on the following passage by Fr. Henri Nouwen. Consider your own death, as well as Jesus' on the cross.

We all must die. And we all will die alone. No one can make that final journey with us. We have to let go of what is most our own and trust that we did not live in vain. Somehow, dying is the greatest of all human moments because it is the moment in which we are asked to give everything. The way we die has not only much to do with the way we have lived but also with the way those who come after us will live. Jesus' death reveals to us that we do not have to live pretending that death is not something that comes to all of us. As he hangs stretched out between heaven and earth, he asks us to look our mortality straight in the face and trust that death does not have the last word. We can then look at the dying in our world and give them hope; we can hold their dying bodies in our arms and trust that mightier arms than ours will receive them and give them the peace and joy they always desired.

In dying, all of humanity is one. And it was into this dying humanity that God entered so as to give us hope.

—Fr. Henri Nouwen[3]

[3] Henri Nouwen, *Walk With Jesus: Stations of the Cross* (Maryknoll: Orbis Books, 1990), pp. 70–71.

## This Week's Mass Readings:

Monday of Holy Week: Is 42:1-7 • Ps 27:1-3, 13-14 • Jn 12:1-11

Tuesday of Holy Week: Is 49:1-6 • Ps 71:1-6b, 15, 17 • Jn 13:21-33, 36-38

Wednesday of Holy Week: Is 50:4-9 • Ps 69:8-10, 21-22, 31, 33-34 • Mt 26:14-25

Holy Thursday: Ex 12:1-8, 11-14 • Ps 116:12-13, 15-18 • 1 Cor 11:23-26 • Jn 13:1-15

Good Friday: Is 52:13–53:12 • Ps 31:2, 6, 12-13, 15-17, 25 • Heb 4:14-16; 5:7-9 • Jn 18:1–19:42

The best way to close a Scripture discussion is to gather up our thoughts, troubles, fears, and hopes by praying as a group. This week, rather than bringing personal petitions to Jesus, talk to him directly about your experiences during the discussion. You've been meditating together on some of the most compelling texts in the New Testament.

Most of us will have had interior responses from which we could speak to the Lord. Even if your prayer is something as simple as "Jesus, I don't really believe you died for me," giving voice to that opens a space for the Holy Spirit to work within you.

We all fail Jesus and one another at times. Thinking about that today may move you to pray in sorrow for those times. We also feel abandoned by God at times, as Jesus felt on the cross. (His plea, "My God, my God, why has thou forsaken me," appears in Matthew 27:46.)

You can be sure that no matter what you feel or think, you're not the only one. We "find" one another when we honestly share what is on our hearts with God and each other. The light breaks through our isolation in darkness (Week 4), revealing that we are not alone but together, the body of Christ, approaching his everlasting light, one step at a time.

Once everyone has prayed, close with an Our Father or a Glory Be.

**Amen.**

Easter Sunday:
The Resurrection
of the Lord

# A Time to Truly Live

You have been raised
with Christ.
　　　　—Colossians 3:1

Ask someone to pray in their own words, or read aloud the following prayer slowly as others pray along silently. This prayer could also be read by asking half the group to pray a verse, and the other half to pray the next one. Close by saying "Amen" together.

### The Anima Christi of St. Elizabeth Ann Seton

### In the name of the Father, and of the Son, and of the Holy Spirit.

Soul of Jesus, sanctify me.
Blood of Jesus, wash me.

Passion of Jesus, comfort me.
Wounds of Jesus, hide me.

Heart of Jesus, receive me.
Spirit of Jesus, enliven me.

Goodness of Jesus, pardon me.
Beauty of Jesus, draw me.

Humility of Jesus, humble me.
Peace of Jesus, pacify me.

Love of Jesus, inflame me.
Kingdom of Jesus, come to me.

Grace of Jesus, replenish me.
Mercy of Jesus, pity me.

Sanctity of Jesus, sanctify me.
Purity of Jesus, purify me.

Cross of Jesus, support me.
Nails of Jesus, hold me.

Mouth of Jesus, bless me in life, in death,
in time and eternity.
Mouth of Jesus, defend me in the hour of death.

Mouth of Jesus, call me to come to thee.
Mouth of Jesus, receive me with thy saints
in glory evermore. [1]

**Amen.**

---

[1] Taken from "The Anima Christi of St. Elizabeth Seton," Catholic Tradition, http://www.catholictradition.org/Litanies/litany86.htm.

Did anyone attend any of the Triduum services or pray with the daily readings during Holy Week? How was that?

Ask one person to read the Scripture passage aloud.

# John 20:1-9

[1] Now on the first day of the week Mary Mag´dalene came to the tomb early, while it was still dark, and saw that the stone had been taken away from the tomb. [2] So she ran, and went to Simon Peter and the other disciple, the one whom Jesus loved, and said to them, "They have taken the Lord out of the tomb, and we do not know where they have laid him." [3] Peter then came out with the other disciple, and they went toward the tomb. [4] They both ran, but the other disciple outran Peter and reached the tomb first; [5] and stooping to look in, he saw the linen cloths lying there, but he did not go in. [6] Then Simon Peter came, following him, and went into the tomb; he saw the linen cloths lying, [7] and the napkin, which had been on his head, not lying with the linen cloths but rolled up in a place by itself. [8] Then the other disciple, who reached the tomb first, also went in, and he saw and believed; [9] for as yet they did not know the scripture, that he must rise from the dead.

1. What stands out to you from this part of St. John's resurrection story?

2. Why do you think Mary Magdalene went to the tomb that morning? What might she have been feeling?

3. What seems to be Mary's primary concern when she goes to the apostles, and what does that indicate about her expectations on that day?

4. What do Peter and the beloved disciple see when they look in the tomb, and why might St. John name some items twice and make special note of the position of others?

5. What words describe Mary and Peter at the tomb? (The text says that only the beloved disciple "believed.") Let's toss out a few. What words likely described Peter after he left Mary at the tomb?

6. Have you ever felt like Mary or Peter at the tomb, or do you know others who feel this way about Jesus? Would anyone be willing to share?

Ask one person to read the Scripture passage aloud.

# Colossians 3:1-4

¹ If then you have been raised with Christ, seek the things that are above, where Christ is, seated at the right hand of God. ² Set your minds on things that are above, not on things that are on earth. ³ For you have died, and your life is hid with Christ in God. ⁴ When Christ who is our life appears, then you also will appear with him in glory.

7. St. Paul says, "Set your minds on things that are above" instead of "things that are on earth" (verse 2). What earthly things rivet your attention? What do you think would be necessary for you to turn your attention away from these things and toward God?

8. Can anyone think of a person you know whose life appears to be "hid with Christ in God"? What does that look like in this person's way of being in the world?

Ask one person to read the Scripture passage aloud.

# Acts 10:34, 37-43

³⁴ And Peter opened his mouth and said: " . . . ³⁷ [T]he word which was proclaimed throughout all Judea, beginning from Galilee after the baptism which John preached: ³⁸ how God anointed Jesus of Nazareth with the Holy Spirit and with power; how he went about

doing good and healing all that were oppressed by the devil, for God was with him. [39] And we are witnesses to all that he did both in the country of the Jews and in Jerusalem. They put him to death by hanging him on a tree; [40] but God raised him on the third day and made him manifest; [41] not to all the people but to us who were chosen by God as witnesses, who ate and drank with him after he rose from the dead. [42] And he commanded us to preach to the people, and to testify that he is the one ordained by God to be judge of the living and the dead. [43] To him all the prophets bear witness that every one who believes in him receives forgiveness of sins through his name."

9. Would someone be willing to summarize St. Peter's preaching? What would you say are his main points and his overall purpose?

10. How does St. Peter justify his preaching about Jesus (verses 39-41)? What do you think of this reason?

11. Do you think that Peter's reason for witnessing and testifying about Jesus applies to us? Why or why not?

12. Biblical scholars describe short summaries about who Jesus is, what he did, and what it means as the *kerygma,* a Greek term meaning "preaching" of the good news. Has anyone ever tried to preach "good news" to someone else? How did that go?

13. How would you describe the "good news" of Jesus in your own life?

14. Do you think you could share this personal good news with someone? What would be some natural ways that we could share our own good news?

Keep the blessings of your Lenten practices in your life by regularly praying with Scripture and receiving the sacraments. Use the daily readings for your *lectio divina*, or work through a book of the New Testament. Commit that fifteen minutes—1% of your day—and Jesus will change your life. Who doesn't want that!

The "things that are on earth" that St. Paul mentioned to the Colossians (3:2) include old habits and ways of thinking and living that do not lead to the abundant life Jesus came to give us (John 10:10). Too often we feel that joy eludes us because we don't have the relationship with Jesus that opens us to the Holy Spirit's life-transforming power.

A relationship with Jesus grows in the same way all relationships do: through time and conversation. That's what prayer is: conversation with God. Talking to Jesus honestly, sharing your life, and seeking his response will nurture, build, and expand your relationship with God in ways you could never imagine.

A regular prayer life makes a way for the power of the resurrection to fill our lives. It makes it possible to overcome old habits and mind-sets. Prayer is precisely how we can set our minds on what is above—God—rather than the passing things of this life. Habits of sin, the areas of our lives that we haven't surrendered to God, the seeking after what cannot bring happiness—all these are ways we love the darkness rather than the light (Week 4). They keep us from the resurrection life that can make our joy complete (John 15:11).

Seek the power of the resurrection in a new way this year. Pick one part of your life where you feel a pressing need to become a new creation, to let the old fall to the ground, a seed from which something new can be born (Week 5). Commit that part of your life to prayer. Search online to find Scriptures that pertain to that struggle. For example, search "Bible anxiety" or "Bible lust" or "Bible fear" or "Bible depression." Just naming your challenge will give the Holy Spirit an opportunity to work in this area of your life.

This much is certain: you are not the first person who has ever struggled with any challenge you face. Your brothers and sisters in Christ have walked this way before you, and are walking it with you right now. They share Scripture passages on the Web because they want you to have the newness of life they have found.

Pray over one of the Scripture passages you find for a day or two, and then move to the next one. Less is always more when it comes to encountering Christ in the word. Use the guide to *lectio divina* in Appendix B to help you get the most out of prayerful reading. It teaches you how to hear from the Lord through Scripture. *Lectio divina* works!

When you commit to *lectio divina* with the Bible, you open the way in your heart for the Lord to give you "a fresh, spiritual way of thinking" in every area of your life (see Ephesians 4:23). St. Paul assures us that "the weapons of our warfare . . . have divine power to destroy strongholds" (2 Corinthians

10:4). God can bring victory over every challenge you face through your relationship with Jesus, and prayer is how that relationship happens. God will do in you what you can't do on your own.

This beautiful summary of the power of Christ's death and resurrection can help when you need inspiration. Carlo Carretto aimed for a career in politics until the fascists took over the Italian government before World War II. He threw himself into Catholic Action instead, a youth movement that engaged laypeople in advancing the religious and social priorities of the Church. He spent twenty years in a blur of meetings, conferences, and public organizing. Then he left it all to become a contemplative in the desert of North Africa as a Little Brother of Jesus, the community patterned after the way of life of Blessed Charles de Foucauld.

Eventually, Carretto returned to Italy to found a community where laypeople could participate with the brothers in prayer and reflection. He was a popular retreat master and the author of many books, most famously *Letters from the Desert*, which describes his years in an Algerian monastery:

> Real death is separation from God, and this is unbearable; real death is faithlessness, hopelessness and lovelessness. . . .
>
> Real death is the chaos where human beings find themselves when they disobey the Father, it is the tangled web to which they are reduced by their passions, it is the total defeat of all their dreams of greatness, it is the disintegration of their whole personality.

Real death is emptiness, darkness, desolation, despair, hatred, destruction. So . . . Christ agreed to enter this death, into this separation, so as to identify himself with all who were in separation, and to save them.

When he touched the depths of their despair, he announced hope with his resurrection.

When he was immersed in their darkness, he made the brightness of the truth burst forth with his resurrection.

When engulfed by the abyss of their lovelessness, he showed them the infinite joy of resurrection love.

By rising from the dead he made all things new. By rising from the dead he opened new heavens. By rising from the dead he opened new life.

—Carlo Carretto[2]

2  Carlo Carretto, *Carlo Carretto: Selected Writings*, (Orbis: Maryknoll, NY, 1994) p. 147, 8.

At this last meeting, if it feels appropriate, someone could open the prayer with the Sign of the Cross. Then each person could thank God for the blessings they received this Lent and Easter. When people are finished praying and it is silent, the person who opened the prayer could close by reading the following prayer as others pray along silently.

**In the name of the Father, and of the Son, and of the Holy Spirit.**

My Lord God, I have no idea where I am going.
I do not see the road ahead of me.
I cannot know for certain where it will end.
Nor do I really know myself,
and the fact that I think that I am following your will
does not mean that I am actually doing so.
But I believe that the desire to please you does in fact
please you.
And I hope I have that desire in all that I am doing.
I hope that I will never do anything apart from that desire.
And I know that if I do this you will lead me
by the right road,
 though I may know nothing about it.
Therefore will I trust you always
though I may seem to be lost and in the shadow of death.
I will not fear, for you are ever with me,
and you will never leave me to face my perils alone.

—Thomas Merton[1]

**Amen.**

³ Thomas Merton, *Thoughts in Solitude* (New York: Farrar, Straus and Giroux, 1956), p. 79.

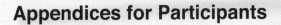

# Appendices for Participants

**A** Small Group Discussion Guide

**B** A Guide to Seeking God in Prayer and Scripture

**C** St. Ignatius and the Two Standards

**D** A Guide to the Sacrament of Reconciliation

Appendix  A

A small group seeks to foster an honest exploration of Jesus Christ with one another. For many, this will be a new experience. You may be wondering what will take place. Will I fit in? Will I even want to come back?

Here are some expectations and values to help participants understand how small groups work as well as what makes them work and what doesn't. When a group meets for the first time, the facilitator may want to read the following aloud and discuss it to be sure people understand small group parameters.

## Purpose

We gather as searchers. Our express purpose for being here is to explore together what it means to live the gospel of Jesus Christ in and through the Church.

## Priority

In order to reap the full fruit of this personal and communal journey, each one of us will make participation in the weekly gatherings a priority.

## Participation

We will strive to create an environment in which all are encouraged to share at their comfort level.

We will begin and end all sessions in prayer, exploring different ways to pray together over time. We will discuss a Scripture passage at every meeting. Participants do not need to read the passage beforehand—no one needs to know anything about the Bible in order to participate. The point is to discuss the text and see how it applies to our own lives.

## Discussion Guidelines

The purpose of our gathering time is to share in "Spirit-filled" discussion. This type of dialogue occurs when the presence of the Holy Spirit is welcomed and encouraged by the nature and tenor of the discussion. To help this happen, we will observe the following guidelines:

- Participants strive always to be respectful, humble, open, and honest in listening and sharing: they don't interrupt, respond abruptly, condemn what another says, or even judge in their hearts.

- Participants share at the level that is comfortable for them personally.

- Silence is a vital part of the experience. Participants are given time to reflect before discussion begins. Keep in mind that a period of comfortable silence often occurs between individuals speaking.

- Participants are enthusiastically encouraged to share while at the same time exercising care to permit others (especially the quieter members) an opportunity to speak. Each participant should aim to maintain a balance: participating without dominating the conversation.

- Participants keep confidential anything personal that may be shared in the group.

- Perhaps most important, participants should cultivate attentiveness to the Holy Spirit's desire to be present in the time spent together. When the conversation seems to need help, ask for the Holy Spirit's intercession silently in your heart. When someone is speaking of something painful or difficult, pray that the Holy Spirit comforts that person. Pray for the Spirit to aid the group in responding sensitively and lovingly. If someone isn't participating, praying for that person during silence may be more helpful than a direct question. These are but a few examples of the ways in which each person might personally invoke the Holy Spirit.

### Time

We meet weekly because that is the best way to become comfortable together, but we can schedule our meetings around any breaks or holidays when many people will be away.

It is important that our group start and end on time. Generally a group meets for about ninety minutes, with an additional thirty minutes or so afterward for refreshments. Agree on these times as a group and work to honor them.

Appendix

## The 1% Challenge™:
## Fifteen Minutes a Day with God's Word

1% of your day is fourteen minutes and
twenty-four seconds.
How you spend that time could change your life!

*Unless you are convinced that prayer is the best use of
your time, you will never find time to pray.*
*—Fr. Hilary Ottensmeyer, OSB[1]*

### If only I had the time!

Time—we only have so much of it each day. All kinds of demands chip away the hours. Modern communication and social media increase our sense of urgency. No wonder we experience conflicting desires over how to spend our time.

One thing we all know for certain: relationships require time. Friendships don't form or last unless people spend time together. Marriages struggle when spouses don't make time to talk and listen deeply to one another. Parents who do not prioritize spending time with their children risk painfully regretting that decision down the road.

Some things never change. We were made for relationships, and relationships take time.

---

[1] Accessed at http://www.saintmeinrad.edu/seminary-blog/echoes-from-the-bell-tower/posts/2015/monastic-time.

## So how about our relationship with God?

Just as all relationships require time, so too does a deepening friendship with God. What kind of relationship do you have with the person in your neighborhood with whom you've never had a personal conversation? Even if you take out her garbage can weekly because she is disabled, she is an acquaintance, not a friend. Friends spend time together. Jesus called us his friends (John 15:15).

One way we spend time with Jesus is at Mass. This will always be the center, source, and summit of our prayer lives. But without personal time with Jesus outside liturgies, the encounter at Mass can resemble meeting that neighbor at a block party: talking for a few minutes without any deep connection. The mysterious reality of that person remains remote.

## How much time should I spend in personal prayer?

A little goes a long way with God.

*Take the 1% Challenge™: for thirty days, spend at least fifteen minutes a day with God and God's word.*

*If you do, you'll never want to stop.*

We've seen it happen again and again. When people build a habit of talking and listening to God, they experience the fruits of a real relationship with Jesus. You, too, can

- begin to know the Lord in ways that affect you personally;
- grow in your ability to hear God's voice and follow his gentle guidance;

- experience more of the Lord's love, peace, and joy—even in difficult circumstances;
- become more attentive to other people, because in prayer, Christ gives us his compassion for every person.

It is not easy, at least not at first. But prayer begets prayer. As you experience the fruit of a deeper friendship with the Lord, your desire for God grows. Your heart longs more and more to *build your life around prayer* rather than just *squeezing it in*.

## How should I spend my fifteen minutes?

Always begin by recognizing that God is with you, even when you're not paying attention. When you attend to God, you are simply focusing on reality.

St. Teresa of Avila called prayer "an intimate sharing between friends."[2] Any good friendship involves three things: talking, listening, and simply being together.

### 1. Talk to God

There is no wrong way to talk to God. Talk about anything on your mind. Keep it real; don't just say what you think a prayerful person should say or what you think God wants to hear. Even saying, "Lord, help me to pray" is itself a prayer.

Keep in mind the first three things we all learn to say as children: *"Thank you," "I'm sorry,"* and *"Please."* That's a great outline for a chat with God!

---

[2] Teresa of Avila, *The Book of Her Life*, trans. with notes by Kieran Kavanaugh, OCD, and Otilio Rodriguez, OCD (Indianapolis/Cambridge : Hacket Publishing, 2008), p. 44.

*2. Listen to God*

> *"Morning after morning he opens my ear that I may hear." (cf. Isaiah 50:4)*

No matter how impossible it may seem, you can learn to hear the Lord's voice in your life. Remember the promise of Jesus: "My sheep hear my voice, and I know them, and they follow me" (John 10:27). Jesus means what he says—this is attainable!

The fastest way to learn to recognize the voice of God is to read the Scriptures prayerfully. With the Holy Spirit coming to our aid, the word becomes "a life-giving encounter" (St. John Paul II, *Novo Millennio Ineunte*, 39). The simple outline of *lectio divina* that follows will help you find what the Lord wants to say to you.

*3. Be with God*

Sometimes words get in the way of deeper communication. St. John of the Cross said, "The Father spoke one Word, which was his Son, and this Word he speaks always in eternal silence, and in silence must it be heard by the soul."[3] The Lord says, "Be still, and know that I am God" (Psalm 46:10).

Begin and end each prayer time with a minute or two of silence to rest in God's presence.

You probably won't hear anything audible or even sense anything interiorly, but be confident that God is filling that silence in ways you cannot immediately perceive. Often something can become very clear later in the day after a time of silence in the morning.

---

[3] *The Collected Works of St. John of the Cross,* trans. by Kieran Kavanaugh, OCD and Otilio Rodriguez, OCD (Washington, DC: ICS Publications, 2010), 92.

## Putting it All Together: *Lectio Divina*

I would like in particular to recall and recommend the ancient tradition of *Lectio divina:* the diligent reading of Sacred Scripture accompanied by prayer brings about that intimate dialogue in which the person reading hears God who is speaking, and in praying, responds to him with trusting openness of heart (*cf. Dei Verbum,* 25). If it is effectively promoted, this practice will bring to the Church—I am convinced of it—a new spiritual springtime.

—Pope Benedict XVI[4]

One of the best ways to "talk," "listen," and "be with" God in a single sitting is the time-honored method of praying with Scripture called *lectio divina* (Latin for "divine reading"). Four "Rs" are an easy way to remember how to do it.

First, **prepare.** Use a Bible; it's less distracting than a phone or device. Begin with the Sign of the Cross. Take a moment to be quiet and still. Ask the Holy Spirit to guide your time.

1. **Read** the Scripture selection slowly and attentively. Note any word, phrase, or image that catches your attention. It's helpful to read the passage more than once, and/or out loud.

2. **Reflect.** Think about the meaning of whatever caught your attention. The Holy Spirit drew you to it for a reason.

[4] Address to Participants in the International Congress Organized to Commemorate the 40th Anniversary of the Dogmatic Constitution on Divine Revelation *(Dei Verbum)*, September 16, 2005. Accessed at www.vatican.va, https://w2.vatican.va/content/benedict-xvi/en/speeches/2005/september/documents/hf_ben-xvi_spe_20050916_40-dei-verbum.html.

What line of thought do you pursue in response? Notice any questions that arise or any emotions you experience. Return to the text as often as you wish.

3. **Respond.** Talk to God about the passage, your thoughts, or anything else on your heart. Thank him for blessings received. Ask him for your own needs as well as those of others. Note any changes or actions you want to make. If the Holy Spirit leads you to any resolution or application in your life, writing it down will help you remember. Ask God to help you to live it out.

4. **Rest**. Rest a few minutes in silence with the Lord. "Be still, and know that I am God" (Psalm 46:10).

## Recommended Scripture Passages for Lectio Divina

Choose passages that are relatively short. The goal is not to cover a lot of material but to listen "with the ear of our heart," as St. Benedict instructed his monks in his *Rule*.

- Read the Gospel passage of the day for the Mass, found online at http://www.usccb.org/nab.

- Slowly work through a Gospel or an epistle, such as Ephesians, Philippians, James, or 1 John.

- Read the psalms.

- Use a Bible app or search online to find reading plans or Scripture passages on topics relevant to your life, such as gratitude, fear, or courage. We're often most attuned to hearing God on topics very important to us personally.

- Many mobile apps will guide you through fifteen minutes of prayer for your 1% time slot. One we especially love is called "Pray as You Go." It uses one of the daily Mass readings from the Scriptures to lead you through a contemplative time.

- Try the EC's thirty-day Kickstart! For a printable copy of thirty Gospel references aimed at getting to know Jesus better, go to www.evangelicalcatholic.org/30-day-kickstart.

**Take the Pledge!**
Join a growing number of people around the country committing to daily prayer: www.evangelicalcatholic.org/onepercent.

**Tips and Further Resources**
For ideas on growing in daily prayer and overcoming obstacles, see www.evangelicalcatholic.org/tips-for-daily-prayer/.

*We only devote periods of quiet time to the things or the people whom we love; and here we are speaking of the God whom we love, a God who wishes to speak to us.*
—Pope Francis[5]

*My secret is simple. I pray.*
—St. Teresa of Calcutta[6]

[5] *The Joy of the Gospel*, 146.
[6] *The Power of Prayer* (New York: MJF Books, 1998), 3, 7–8, quoted in *United States Catholic Catechism for Adults* (Washington, DC: United States Conference of Catholic Bishops, 2006), p. 479.

# Appendix C

Composed in the sixteenth century by St. Ignatius of Loyola, founder of the Jesuit order, the "Two Standards" is a well-known spiritual exercise that can help you choose light over darkness.[1]

Ignatius spent his early adulthood in the military and was known as a vain, rough-and-tumble adventurer. A cannon ball hit him during a battle, seriously injuring his leg and leaving him bedridden for months. When he saw it healing in an unattractive fashion, he ordered it re-broken and set again. This in the age before anesthesia!

Reading for entertainment during many of his months of recuperation, Ignatius noticed something. When he read adventure stories and romances, he was engaged, but the excitement faded fast. He quickly found himself uninterested, dissatisfied, and agitated. On the other hand, if he read about Jesus or the lives of the saints, his interest continued, along with peace and a desire to serve God. This led to a spiritual conversion.

Ignatius left his home and became a begging pilgrim. He also began guiding people through spiritual exercises using Scripture. From this work, he composed his *Spiritual Exercises* to help people more deeply appreciate the state of the world, what they themselves are really like, and what God wants for

[1] St. Ignatius of Loyola, "The Fourth Day, Meditation on Two Standards" in *Spiritual Exercises of St. Ignatius of Loyola*, trans. Fr. Elder Mullan, SJ (New York: P. J. Kenedy & Sons, 1914), http://www.ccel.org/ccel/ignatius/exercises.xiii.v.html.

them. The "Two Standards" is one of these exercises. Ignatius asks us to imagine the forces of good and evil as armies, each gathered under its own flag, or "standard." The army of darkness and the army of light stand opposed on the field of battle. Which side will you stand with?

Ignatius was convinced that the imagination holds a privileged place in the life of prayer. By imagining ourselves in the Scripture stories, or imagining ourselves in situations such as a battle of light and darkness, we give God the opportunity to communicate with us through our feelings and thoughts. At first, imagining a scene may feel more like something you are just making up yourself than something inspired by God. Don't let this discourage you! You will soon start to notice moments when unexpected ideas occur or feelings emerge. That is the Holy Spirit acting in your heart!

Don't let concern over imagining the landscape and characters obscure your interior life. It's your own heart you are really exploring. Ask yourself, "Where is there darkness and where is there light? In what ways do I choose evil over good?"

Ignatius believed people should be given spiritual exercises by a spiritual director. This written version is a compromise, but if you enter it asking God to guide you, the Holy Spirit will be your director. Someday you may want to seek a Jesuit or Ignatian-trained spiritual director to lead you through the entire Exercises. It's a blessed experience that produces great fruit long after the retreat is over.

### Before Beginning
Set aside twenty to thirty minutes in a place you won't be interrupted. Read through the whole exercise first to familiarize yourself

with the material. This will allow you to move through it with less intellectual concentration. Try to spend most of the prayer time imagining, not concentrating, on the text. The steps are numbered to make this easier. (This is not the same numbering used in the original meditation.)

## Collect Yourself and Prepare

Begin your prayer by placing yourself in God's presence.

Take a few deep breaths and remember that God is closer to you than you are to yourself. He suffers none of the illusions to which we are subject, and he looks on us with love, as his children, rather than through the prism of the world.

Ask God for the grace to focus on the feelings the Holy Spirit draws to your attention during this exercise.

Ask the Spirit to reveal to you any tendencies you may have had in the past when choosing between darkness and light. Ask him to show you times when you chose one or the other.

Thank God for any blessings he will give you in this time.

## Engage Your Imagination

1. Imagine Jesus Christ and his followers on a glistening green plain where brightly colored tents have been pitched and flags billow in the breeze. Look across the field. Allow yourself to respond emotionally to this sight.

2. Now look into the distance. Imagine Satan with his followers in a deep ravine, all grays and shadows, and the air dead still. Allow yourself to respond emotionally to this sight as well.

3. Ask God to give you the courage to see clearly the face of good and the face of evil.

4. Envision the commanders on both fields of battle.
   - See Jesus as the supreme Commander-in-Chief in the fields of Jerusalem.
   - See the enemy of our human nature, Ignatius' description of Satan, in a Babylonian field—whatever a field of an enemy looks like to you.

5. Ask God to give you knowledge of how Satan deceives you; Jesus calls him the "Father of lies" (John 8:44). Pray that you will be guarded against these lies.

6. Ask for knowledge of the true life that the supreme loving Commander shows as well as the grace to imitate him.

7. Imagine the chief of the enemy seated in that great field of Babylon, as in a great chair of fire and smoke, horrible and terrifying.
   - Consider how he summons innumerable demons that he will scatter forth to do his work: some to one city and others to another, and so throughout the world, until they are in every location on earth.
   - Consider how he instructs them, how he tells them to cast out nets and chains.
   - Hear him encouraging his demons to first tempt with a longing for riches, that men and women who gain them may more easily be pumped up with pride by what they own, rather than who they are (vain honor).

- From these three vices, riches, vain honor, and pride, men and women are drawn to all the rest.

8. Now turn to Christ's army. Consider how our Lord puts himself in a lowly place, beautiful and attractive.
   - Consider how the Lord of the entire universe chooses so many persons—apostles, disciples, etc.—and sends them through all the world spreading love and hope to every kind of person: married, single, rich, poor, old, young, laborer, executive.
   - Consider Jesus instructing his servants and friends sent on this expedition, encouraging a desire to help all.
   - See the insults and contempt that the followers of our Lord encounter. From these humility follows.
   - In comparison with Lucifer's armies, there are three means of forming followers: the first, poverty against riches; the second, insults or contempt against worldly honor; the third, humility against pride. From these three come all the other virtues.

9. The following questions may help your meditation. Move on if they don't.
   - Ask Jesus to teach you how his mind works.
   - Ask him to help you see how people who have chosen the light make their decisions.
   - Ask God what these people value and how this guides their choices.

10. After you have imagined all these things, ask Mary, Jesus' mother, and any of your favorite saints to intercede for you.
- Ask Jesus, the Father, and the Holy Spirit to help you learn whatever it is God wants to teach you from this meditation.

Rest with God in your thoughts and feelings. Close by thanking God for any insights you received. Ask God to continue to unfold the graces he wants you to receive from this meditation, and for your heart to be receptive to them.

Appendix **D**

If it has been a long time since you last went to Confession—or if you've never been—you may be hesitant and unsure. Don't let these very common feelings get in your way. Reconciling with God and the Church always brings great joy. Take the plunge—you will be glad you did!

If it will help to alleviate your fears, familiarize yourself with the step-by-step description of the process below. Most priests are happy to help anyone willing to take the risk. If you forget anything, the priest will remind you. So don't worry about committing every step and word to memory. Remember, Jesus isn't giving you a test; he just wants you to experience the grace of his mercy!

Catholics believe that the priest acts *in persona Christi,* "in the person of Christ." The beauty of the sacraments is that they touch us both physically and spiritually. On the physical level in Confession, we hear the words of absolution through the person of the priest. On the spiritual level, we know that it is Christ assuring us that he has truly forgiven us. We are made clean!

You usually have the option of going to Confession anonymously—in a confessional booth or in a room with a screen—or face-to-face with the priest. Whatever you prefer will be fine with the priest.

**Steps in the Sacrament of Reconciliation:**

1. Prepare to receive the sacrament by praying and examining your conscience. If you need help, you can find many different lists of questions online that will help you examine your conscience.

2. Once you're with the priest, begin by making the Sign of the Cross while greeting the priest with these words: "Bless me, Father, for I have sinned." Then tell him how long it has been since your last confession. If it's your first confession, tell him so.

3. Confess your sins to the priest. If you are unsure about anything, ask him to help you. Place your trust in God, who is a merciful and loving Father.

4. When you are finished, indicate this by saying, "I am sorry for these and all of my sins." Don't worry later that you forgot something. This closing statement covers everything that didn't come to mind in the moment. Trust God that he has brought to mind what he wants you to address.

5. The priest will assign you a penance, such as a prayer, a Scripture reading, or a work of mercy, service, or sacrifice.

6. Express sorrow for your sins by saying an Act of Contrition. Many versions of this prayer can be found online. If memorization is difficult for you, just say you're sorry in your own words.

7. The priest, acting in the person of Christ, will absolve you of your sins with prayerful words, ending with "I absolve you from your sins in the name of the Father, and of the Son, and of the

Holy Spirit." You respond by making the Sign of the Cross and saying, "Amen."

8. The priest will offer some proclamation of praise, such as "Give thanks to the Lord, for he is good" (from Psalm 136). You can respond, "His mercy endures forever."

9. The priest will dismiss you.

10. Be sure to complete your assigned penance immediately or as soon as possible.

# Appendices for Facilitators

**E** The Role of a Facilitator

**F** A Guide for Each Session of *With Jesus to the Cross: Year B*

**G** Leading Prayer and "Connection to the Cross This Week"

Appendix

Perhaps no skill is more important to the success of a small group than the ability to facilitate a discussion lovingly. It is God's Holy Spirit working through our personal spiritual journey, not necessarily our theological knowledge, that makes this possible.

The following guidelines can help facilitators avoid some of the common pitfalls of small group discussion. The goal is to open the door for the Spirit to take the lead and guide your every response because you are attuned to his movements.

Pray daily and before your small group meeting. This is the only way you can learn to sense the Spirit's gentle promptings when they come!

### You Are a Facilitator, Not a Teacher

As a facilitator, it can be extremely tempting to answer every question. You may have excellent answers and be excited about sharing them with your brothers and sisters in Christ. However, a more Socratic method, by which you attempt to draw answers from participants, is much more fruitful for everyone else and for you as well.

Get in the habit of reflecting participants' questions or comments to the whole group before offering your own input. It is not necessary for you as a facilitator to enter immediately into the discussion or to offer a magisterial answer. When others have sufficiently addressed an issue, try to exercise restraint in your comments. Simply affirm what has been said; then thank them and move on.

If you don't know the answer to a question, have a participant look it up in the *Catechism of the Catholic Church* and read it aloud to the group. If you cannot find an answer, ask someone to research the question for the next session. Never feel embarrassed to say, "I don't know." Simply acknowledge the quality of the question and offer to follow up with that person after you have done some digging. Remember, you are a facilitator, not a teacher.

## Affirm and Encourage

We are more likely to repeat a behavior when it is openly encouraged. If you want more active participation and sharing, give positive affirmation to the responses of the group members. This is especially important if people are sharing from their hearts. A simple "Thank you for sharing that" can go a long way in encouraging further discussion in your small group.

If someone has offered a theologically questionable response, don't be nervous or combative. Wait until others have offered their input. It is very likely that someone will proffer a more helpful response, which you can affirm by saying something such as "That is the Christian perspective on that topic. Thank you."

If no acceptable response is given and you know the answer, exercise great care and respect in your comments so as not to appear smug or self-righteous. You might begin with something such as "Those are all interesting perspectives. What the Church has said about this is . . . "

## Avoid Unhelpful Tangents

Nothing can derail a Spirit-filled discussion more quickly than digressing on unnecessary tangents. Try to keep the session on track. If conversation strays from the topic, ask yourself, "Is this a

Spirit-guided tangent?" Ask the Holy Spirit too! If not, bring the group back by asking a question that steers conversation to the Scripture passage or to a question you have been discussing. You may even suggest kindly, "Have we gotten a little off topic?" Most participants will respond positively and get back on track through your sensitive leading.

That being said, some tangents may be worth pursuing if you sense a movement of the Spirit. It may be exactly where God wants to steer the discussion. You will find that taking risks can yield some beautiful results.

### Don't Fear the Silence

Be okay with silence. Most people need a moment or two to come up with a response to a question. People naturally require some time to formulate their thoughts and put them into words. Some may need a few moments just to gather the courage to speak at all.

Regardless of the reason, don't be afraid of a brief moment of silence after asking a question. Let everyone in the group know early on that silence is an integral part of normal small group discussion. They needn't be anxious or uncomfortable when it happens. God works in silence!

This applies to times of prayer as well. If no one shares or prays after a sufficient amount of time, just move on gracefully.

### The Power of Hospitality

A little hospitality can go far in creating community. Everyone likes to feel cared for. This is especially true in a small group whose purpose is to connect to Jesus Christ, a model for care, support, and compassion.

Make a point to greet people personally when they first arrive. Ask them how their day has been going. Take some time to invest in the lives of your small group participants. Pay particular attention to newcomers. Work at remembering each person's name. Help everyone feel comfortable and at home. Allow your small group to be an environment in which authentic relationships take shape and blossom.

### Encourage Participation

Help everyone to get involved, especially those who are naturally less vocal or outgoing. To encourage participation initially, always invite various group members to read aloud the selected readings. Down the road, even after the majority of the group feels comfortable sharing, you may still have some quieter members who rarely volunteer a response to a question but would be happy to read.

### Meteorology?

Keep an eye on the "Holy Spirit barometer." Is the discussion pleasing to the Holy Spirit? Is this conversation leading participants to a deeper personal connection to Jesus Christ? The intellectual aspects of our faith are certainly important to discuss, but conversation can sometimes degenerate into an unedifying showcase of intellect and ego. Other times discussion becomes an opportunity for gossip, detraction, complaining, or even slander. When this happens, you can almost feel the Holy Spirit leaving the room!

If you are aware that this dynamic has taken over a discussion, take a moment to pray quietly in your heart. Ask the Holy Spirit to help you bring the conversation to a more wholesome topic. This can often be achieved simply by moving to the next question.

## Pace

Generally, you want to pace the session to finish in the allotted time, but sometimes this may be impossible without sacrificing quality discussion. If you reach the end of your meeting and find that you have covered only half the material, don't fret! This is often the result of lively Spirit-filled discussion and meaningful theological reflection.

In such a case, you may take time at another meeting to cover the remainder of the material. If you have only a small portion left, you can ask participants to pray through these on their own and come to the following meeting with any questions or insights they may have. Even if you must skip a section to end on time, make sure you leave adequate time for prayer and to review the "Connection to the Cross This Week" section. This is vital in helping participants integrate their discoveries from the group into their daily lives.

## Genuine Friendships

The best way to show Jesus' love and interest in your small group members is to meet with them for coffee, dessert, or a meal outside of your small group time.

You can begin by suggesting that the whole group get together for ice cream or some other social event at a different time than when your group usually meets. Socializing will allow relationships to develop. It provides the opportunity for different kinds of conversations than small group sessions allow. You will notice an immediate difference in the quality of community in your small group at the next meeting.

After that first group social, try to meet one-on-one with each person in your small group. This allows for more indepth conversation and personal sharing, giving you the chance to know each participant better so that you can love and care for each one as Jesus would.

Jesus called the twelve apostles in order that they could "be with him" (Mark 3:14). When people spend time together, eat together, laugh together, cry together, and talk about what matters to them, intense Christian community develops. That is the kind of community Jesus was trying to create, and that must be the kind of community we try to create, because it changes lives. And changed lives change the world!

## Joy

Remember that seeking the face of the Lord brings joy! Nothing is more fulfilling, more illuminating, and more beautiful than fostering a deep and enduring relationship with Jesus Christ. Embrace your participants and the entire spiritual journey with a spirit of joyful anticipation of what God wants to accomplish.

> *"These things I have spoken to you, that my joy may be in you, and that your joy may be full." (John 15:11)*

# Appendix (F)

These notes assist leaders in tailoring sessions to the needs of your specific group. They include historical information on biblical times that may be relevant in some circumstances but not others, and suggest ways to help your group become comfortable together and grow as a spiritually seeking community.

God can respond to us personally through the Scriptures, whether or not we know anything about the history of the ancient Near East. However, commonly known information about the social and religious situations in the era when Jesus lived can sometimes be the way that the Holy Spirit leads us to what he wants us to discuss. Sometimes a brief summary of a few facts will help your group better understand the Scripture you're discussing.

We also give you easy-to-find online resources where you can research such material yourself should you ever lead a Scripture discussion group without the aid of a guide. And although there is no specifically Catholic online Bible dictionary or commentary, you can always type in "Catholic interpretation" before the topic you are researching, and many websites will appear. Make sure you find ones that are reliable and are written by scholars with good credentials.

Some of these historical and religious details are fascinating, but always resist any urge to teach too much rather than facilitate conversation. The information we provide will be relevant and helpful to the conversation in some circumstances and not in others. When a few facts would add clarity and illuminate a discussion, share briefly—ideally, in your own words—and then ask a question about how this information can deepen our understanding of what was happening and what it means for us today. In other words, give the conversation back to the group as quickly as possible.

Some of the session notes pertain to the needs of a group at a particular time in its development. The notes for the first week include suggestions on ways to make people feel comfortable, while the notes for the last week suggest ideas for encouraging participants to go forward into a deepening life in Christ. Review the guide for each session as you prepare weekly. Jot down some notes so you can summarize the information in your own words should that be appropriate.

To help your group succeed, let this principle guide every meeting: the most important priority for a small group discussion is to follow the Spirit's leading, not to cover all the material. Sometimes God may want to speak to your group through only one reading. Go with it! If the Spirit leads, the discussion will enrich the group far more than a rush through all the material.

Regarding when to begin your Lenten study, many groups gather the week before Ash Wednesday so that people can get to know one another without also trying to cram in a Scripture discussion. We highly recommend this, if possible. Books can be distributed or sold at this meeting. You could ask people to bring food or drink to make socializing easier, or provide it yourself. During introductions, ask people to share their name and other relevant details (residence hall at college and hometown, years in a parish or neighborhood, family details, and so forth). To help people open up a little, ask them, "Why did you sign up (or come to) this group? What are your hopes?"

## First Sunday of Lent: A Time to Change

Allow a little extra time for introductions if this is the first meeting. This is more important than covering all the material.

*Opening Prayer:* For this first meeting, it would be ideal to pray a short, simple extemporaneous prayer asking God to bless your time together at this meeting and through the coming weeks. You could also ask God to make the meetings fruitful for everyone present.

Praying extemporaneously models for the participants how to speak directly to God. If you don't usually pray aloud in your own words, practice by doing it during your personal prayer time. Become accustomed to talking to God on your own, and you will become comfortable doing it with others. For more on leading prayer, see Appendix G.

*Question 3:* Allow people to share what they know or guess about the meaning of "covenant" before providing information. Use your own words rather than reading these descriptions.

The explanation for "covenant" below comes from Bible Odyssey, the online Bible dictionary from the Society of Biblical Literature (SBL). Its academic approach to the material makes it a very helpful resource whenever you have a question on facts about the various groups, social situations, and other details of the ancient Near East."[1]

[1] Bible Odyssey "About Us" page: https://www.bibleodyssey.org/about-us. SBL describes itself as "the oldest and largest learned society devoted to the critical investigation of the Bible based on the Humanities' core disciplines. With over eight thousand members worldwide, it represents and convenes scholars whose life work is in biblical and ancient Near Eastern studies. The SBL promotes the academic study of the Bible and of sacred texts generally."

In the Hebrew Bible, the covenant (Hebrew: *berit*) is the formal agreement between Yhwh and the people of Israel and Judah, in which each agrees to a set of obligations toward the other. The language and understanding of covenant is based on ancient Near Eastern treaties between nations.

The Bible understands covenant from two different perspectives. The unconditional or eternal covenant (Hebrew *berit´ olam*) between Yhwh and Israel/Judah presumes that the covenant can never be broken, although it does allow for divine judgment.[2]

*Connection to Christ:* Questions on the reading from 1 Peter appear in this section because you won't have time to discuss all three readings for this coming Sunday's liturgy, especially if this is your first meeting. Introductions will take time. Questions on this reading are unlikely to come up this week but may next week when you ask about their experience with the prayer exercises.

St. Peter says that Jesus "preached to the spirits in prison" (1 Peter 3:19). No questions are asked about this verse because many just find it confusing. Much ink has been spilled speculating about it. The official position of the Church is that Jesus went to deceased human beings to proclaim the good news and to free the righteous people who had gone before him. Only proffer this information if asked or if it seems necessary. (The *Catechism's* teaching on when Jesus "descended into hell"—a line from the Apostles' Creed—is in paragraphs 632–633).

---

[2] "Covenant in the Hebrew Bible" by Marvin A. Sweeney, Professor, Claremont School of Theology, https://www.bibleodyssey.org/en/passages/related-articles/covenant-in-the-hebrew-bible.

## Second Sunday of Lent: A Time to Listen

*Opening and Closing Prayers:* Open and close with extemporaneous prayer, if possible. If not, use those provided. The closing instructions allow time for people to voice their needs. Praying the closing prayer extemporaneously allows you to gather up all that has happened during your conversation in a way that a written prayer never could, no matter how beautiful or profound.

*Opening Discussion*: See the notes for the First Sunday of Lent on the reading from 1 Peter that "Jesus preached to the spirits in prison."

*Question 5:* Paragraph 555 of the *Catechism of the Catholic Church* explains how the Church understands the appearance of Moses and Elijah at the Transfiguration. Use this explanation only if your group needs more information or clarification on what the Church believes.

*Question 9:* This question includes many additional questions. To make it more fruitful, you may want to set people up to listen and respond. Here is one way, but say what comes naturally:

This question has lots of additional questions within it, so I'm going to read it really slowly. I'll pause in the middle before the concluding question to give you time to think about the first part. Then I'll pause again to give you more time to think at the end. After that, I'll ask if anyone is willing to share their thoughts on this topic. If you want me to repeat anything, just ask.

You may not have time to read and discuss Thomas Keating's thoughts on the Transfiguration during the meeting. If you don't, ask your group to read it at home. Encourage them to read it by telling the group it will be discussed during the opening discussion at the next meeting.

## Third Sunday of Lent: A Time to Believe

*Opening Discussion:* A prompt question on the Keating reading is offered in case you didn't have time to read and discuss the excerpt during the last session. Skip it if you did discuss it.

Both readings discussed in this session allude to signs. Some Scripture passages indicate good reasons to ask for a sign; others indicate bad reasons. You wouldn't want anyone to leave with the impression that the Bible insists it is never acceptable to ask for a sign, or that it always is. The *Catechism of the Catholic Church* says humans need signs.[3] Explore the subject to help people realize that though Jesus seems to condemn asking for a sign in the Gospel reading, he may have been addressing those people's motive rather than the inherent worth of seeking signs.

*Questions 12 and 13:* These questions ask people to think about their own ways of responding to God—potentially an important

---

[3] Paragraph 1146, *Signs of the human world*: "In human life, signs and symbols occupy an important place. As a being at once body and spirit, man expresses and perceives spiritual realities through physical signs and symbols. As a social being, man needs signs and symbols to communicate with others, through language, gestures, and actions. The same holds true for his relationship with God."

topic for your group. Some people tend so strongly to intellectual analysis or historical facts that the sharing of personal experiences is inhibited, both by the person with that propensity and by others in the group who don't feel as "smart" or well-informed.

Ideally, this question will help group members to identify their own tendencies for themselves. You shouldn't point out someone else's behavior, nor should anyone else. You might want to speak about yourself first to model vulnerability. If a group member starts talking about what *someone else* does, reign in the commentator as quickly and gently as possible. Point out that we should all speak only for ourselves.

Your response to anyone's recognition of their own tendencies should always be loving and positive. For example, if someone says, "Yeah, I know I always want to talk about theology [or history or Church controversies] too much," you could respond, "It's really helpful to me when I become aware of something about myself. It seems like God can do more in me when that happens. Maybe that's because he's the one who helped that knowledge break through to me."

*Connection to the Cross This Week:* Encourage the group to read Exodus 20:1-17 on their own before the weekend Mass and to commit to praying fifteen minutes on three days. If time allows, briefly share blessings you receive from praying regularly.

*Closing Prayer:* The instructions ask the group members to speak to God directly about their needs as part of their prayer rather than listing their needs for you or for someone else to lift up to the Lord. Talking to God in front of other people will be entirely new for many. You will need to allow long pauses and periods of silence for people to gather their thoughts. For more on helping people pray aloud together, read Appendix G: Leading Prayer and "Connection to the Cross This Week."

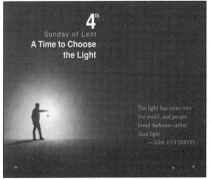

The light has come into the world, and people loved darkness rather than light.
—John 3:19 (NRSV)

## Fourth Sunday of Lent: A Time to Choose the Light

*Opening Prayer:* Before the meeting, ask a group member to prepare for the leader's role for this opening prayer. If you think that would burden any person you ask, read it aloud yourself after prayerful preparation. This is a moving tale of sorrow and loss that deserves advance preparation.

*Opening Discussion:* If it appears people aren't praying on their own using the "Connection to the Cross" suggestions, you could witness to the fruits of your experience from spending fifteen minutes with God during the day and praying with the suggested Scripture passages. Alternatively, you could describe how considering the questions on the reading that wasn't discussed during the meeting made it more meaningful during Sunday Mass.

Witnessing is well worth the time. People sometimes respond and try new things when they hear the benefits that others experience. This is one reason the Opening Discussion asks about people's experiences at the beginning of each meeting.

*Question 9:* This Sunday the Church pairs Old Testament readings about the Jewish exile in Babylon with Jesus' teaching that people love the darkness more than the light. Linking images of exile and darkness works spiritually: emotionally, we can easily move between them to understand our inner lives and actions. These images evoke similar feelings of loneliness, isolation, and living far from our true homes. We see that alienation from others, a kind of exile, is the darkness in some people's lives, even if not in our own.

But there are differences as well. As the session explains, the Church understands the exile as a purification for the Israelites who had persistently disobeyed God and disregarded and mocked the prophets God sent to help them (See *Catechism of the Catholic Church,* 710). Darkness in St. John's Gospel, on the other hand, seems to be about what we do that we want to keep secret. We love the darkness that hides our life more than we love the light, Jesus, who illuminates it. The darkness Jesus describes does not purify us as the exile did for the Israelites.

We can understand, however, that the Israelites chose darkness—worshipping false gods and rejecting the prophets God sent to correct them. God allowed the Babylonian conquest that led Israel into the darkness and suffering of exile because of these choices, and used that suffering to purify them.

Suffering always comes from choosing what cannot give life (darkness). Everyone who walks with Christ learns that God does purify us through suffering, especially that which we bring on ourselves. Suffering often breaks us down to a point in which we let God into our lives and hearts. Our defenses drop when we're desperate: we realize independence is a lie and that we desperately need God and other people.

*Connection to the Cross This Week:* Encourage the group to read the material on the Sacrament of Reconciliation. If time allows, very briefly share the fruits you've experienced from Confession. Many Catholics feel great fear and trepidation about this sacrament, which keeps them from the tremendous graces they could be receiving regularly. Your enthusiastic witness to the power of the sacrament in your own life could help someone overcome their own embarrassment and discomfort.

While less important than encouraging the Sacrament of Reconciliation, you might also mention the Two Standards meditation from *The Spiritual Exercises of Ignatius of Loyola*. This will give group members a taste of Ignatian spirituality and a glimpse of the great gift St. Ignatius is to the Church. You could suggest that if enough people try this exercise, the group could share their experience in lieu of the Opening Discussion at the next meeting. If you do, make a note in Week 5 to remind yourself.

*Closing Prayer:* If group members didn't voice needs directly to God last week when it was first suggested, try again this week. Speaking to God together will spiritually form your group as much, and possibly even more, than Scripture discussion. Encourage people in your own words. You could say that no one judges someone in prayer and that we all start somewhere with praying aloud. Witness to any fruits from this way of praying that you've experienced.

## Fifth Sunday of Lent: A Time to Die

*Opening Discussion:* If the majority of people prayed St. Ignatius' meditation on the Two Standards and you discuss it, skip Question 2.

*Questions:* Familiarize yourself well with the questions in this session before your meeting. The questions on the reading of John 12:20-33 sometimes follow up on a previous question. Skip a question if the group has already explored that topic.

## Palm Sunday: A Time to Weep

*Opening Discussion:* Pause for up to a full minute after this question to allow time for people to think, remember, and find words. If no one speaks, you could prime the pump by briefly sharing your own experience of the Passion.

This discussion could become too lengthy. Allow only one or two people to speak. Apologize if others seemed to want to talk. In your own words, suggest something like this:

> We can continue talking about our own experiences of the Passion another time. The reading of the Passion narrative will take more time than usual, even though we won't be reading it all. I'm sorry to cut off such a rich conversation, but I want to make sure we have time to discuss the reading.

For the readings, consider asking a group member or several members to prepare for these readings in advance. Encourage them to practice reading it slowly, allowing time for silence where indicated and wherever else they think appropriate. Advise them to pray over it as well as rehearse it. The Passion of Jesus deserves to be read well and prayerfully!

*Question 11:* No one might want to speculate on what emotions might have been behind Caiaphas' determination that Jesus should die or on the viciousness of the attacks on Jesus. If that is the case, ask questions from people's experience of bullies or of how people with power sometimes treat others at work or elsewhere. People who feel threatened sometimes try to diminish or eliminate the person who threatens them.

If that doesn't go anywhere, proffer a few historical facts. Caiaphas had the longest tenure as high priest in the first century, from 18 BC to 37 AD. He was apparently very successful in working with the Romans, the empire that occupied Israel during Jesus' life (and long afterward as well).[4] Ask, "What would someone whose success depends on the Romans think of indigenous religious movements?"

*Question 13:* Regarding the courage of Joseph of Arimathea, if the dangerous situation of Jesus' followers doesn't come up during the discussion, ask something similar to this in your own words: "What would be the situation of Jesus' friends and followers after the Sanhedrin had given Jesus to the Romans?" Group members should be able to realize the peril that came upon the disciples once their leader was in the hands of the empire. If it doesn't emerge, you could note that the Romans regularly murdered all members of any insurrectionist movement, and then move to the next question. Pontius Pilate likely thought Jesus called himself a king because he was organizing a political rebellion.

---

[4] Joel Marcus, *Mark 8-16: A New Translation with Introduction and Commentary*, The Anchor Yale Bible (Yale University Press: New Haven and London, 2009), p. 1002.

## Easter Sunday: A Time to Truly Live

This is the last meeting of this Lenten small group series. Make it special by asking people to bring treats to eat and drink afterward, or provide these yourself.

Even though this series is ending, your group need not stop meting if members wish to continue. That would be a credit to your ability to facilitate well and foster a loving community through the grace of the Holy Spirit! If you're willing to continue leading, ask the group at this meeting whether they would be interested in meeting for a six-week small group series, perhaps after a break of a few weeks. Find other EC small group guides on our materials page: www.evangelicalcatholic.org/materials, or just search "Evangelical Catholic materials."

Meeting every week is ideal because no one has to remember whether the group meets that week or not, and a month doesn't elapse when someone misses once. However, the group might consider a modified schedule if that would allow people to continue. You could meet every other week, or perhaps meet for three weeks in a row, take a week off, and then meet for another three weeks. The most successful groups, however, meet weekly.

*First Reading from Acts:* This comes from a much larger story. Our questions address Peter preaching the good news because the

Lectionary selected only that portion. You could read Acts 10 to provide more context, but knowledge of the larger context could lead to a tangent and push the session overtime. This session has questions on all three readings, and you will need time to review the "Connection to the Cross for Life" section. Keep the group focused on the "good news" of Jesus death and resurrection, the *kerygma*. Many Christians can't articulate what we believe the good news is! If your group leaves with a stronger sense of what Jesus did and what it means, that would be a beautiful outcome, and far more important for each person's faith than almost anything else could be.

*Question 2:* If no adequate answers surface regarding why Mary Magdalene went to the tomb, ask, "What reasons do we go to a gravesite soon after a death?" This should inform the discussion of what she was feeling.

*Question 8:* If no one can think of a person whose life embodies being "hid with Christ in God," invite the group to speculate about what it would be like if someone were living this way.

*Closing Prayer:* Because this is the last meeting (for Lent at least), make the closing prayer special. The instructions ask everyone to voice thanksgiving for blessings they have received this Lent and Easter. If your group is still shy about praying aloud, pray first yourself to help model the types of things they could say. Review beforehand the "Connection to the Cross for Life" section for ideas about what could help the group members in their spiritual lives, and ask specifically for the blessings people need.

Appendix **G**

**Opening Prayer**

We have provided a guided opening prayer for each session because it can help people who are completely new to small groups and shared extemporaneous prayer feel more at ease. If everyone or most people present are already comfortable speaking to God in their own words aloud in a group, you won't need these prayers at all. It's always better to talk to God from our hearts in a small group. It contributes to the intimacy of the group and also builds individual intimacy with God.

Since some people have never witnessed spontaneous prayer, it's part of your role to model it. Prayers from the heart spoken aloud demonstrate how to talk to God honestly and openly. Seeing someone pray this way expands a person's understanding of who God is and the relationship they can have with Jesus Christ.

You can grow in extemporaneous prayer by praying aloud directly to Jesus during your personal prayer time and as you prepare for the group. This will help "prime the pump," so to speak.

Even if you enjoy praying spontaneously aloud, your goal as a facilitator is to provide opportunities for everyone to grow spiritually. People who pray aloud with others grow in leaps and bounds—we've seen it! After the first meeting, tell the group that you will allow time at the end of your extemporaneous prayer for others to voice prayers. As soon as the group appears to have grown into this, invite other people to open the group with prayer instead of leading it yourself or using the prayer provided.

If you don't do it in the first meeting, in the second week, pray the opening prayer in your own words. Here are some simple parts to include:

1. Praise God! Say what a great and wonderful God our Father is. Borrow language from the psalms of praise if you don't have your own. Just search online for "praise psalms."

2. Thank God! Thank the Lord for the gift of gathering together. Thank him for giving each person present the desire to sacrifice their time to attend the meetings. Thank him for the blessing of your parish or campus community.

3. Ask God for your needs. Ask God to bless your time together and to make it fruitful for all present as well as for his kingdom. Ask Jesus to be with you, who are two or three gathered in his name (Matthew 18:20). Ask the Holy Spirit to open hearts, illuminate minds, and deepen each person's experience of Lent through the Scripture passages you'll read and discuss. Ask the Holy Spirit to guide the discussion so that you can all grow from it.

4. Close by invoking Jesus: "We pray this through Christ our Lord" or "We pray this in Jesus' name."

5. End with the Sign of the Cross.

**Some essentials for extemporaneous prayer:**

- Speak in the first-person plural "we." For example, "Holy Spirit, we ask you to open our hearts . . . " It's fine to add a line asking the Holy Spirit to help you facilitate the discussion as he wills, or something else to that effect, but most of the prayer should be for the whole group.

- Model speaking directly to Jesus our Lord. This may sound obvious, but among Catholic laypeople, it isn't frequently practiced or modeled. This is a very evangelical thing to do in the sense that it witnesses to the gospel. Not only does it show how much we believe that the Lord loves us, but it also demonstrates our confidence that Jesus himself is listening to us! As we say our Lord's name, we remind ourselves, as well as those who hear us, that we aren't just talking to ourselves. This builds up faith.

You and anyone unaccustomed to hearing someone pray to Jesus directly may feel a bit uncomfortable at first. But group members will quickly become more at ease as they hear these prayers repeatedly and experience more intimacy with Jesus. Bear in mind always that many graces come from praying "the name which is above every name" (Philippians 2:9).

If you've never publicly prayed to Jesus, you may feel childish at first, but pray for the humility of a child. After all, Jesus did say that we needed to become like children (Matthew 18:3)! The more we pray directly to Jesus in our personal prayer, the less awkward it will feel when we pray to him publicly.

- Model great faith and trust that the Lord hears your prayer and will answer it. It's terrific just to say in prayer, "Jesus, we trust you!"

- You can always close extemporaneous prayer by inviting the whole group to join in a prayer of the Church, such as the Glory Be, the Our Father, or the Hail Mary. This will bring all into the prayer if previously, just one person was praying aloud extemporaneously.

### Closing Prayer

For the closing prayer, we recommend that you always include extemporaneous prayer, even if you also use the prayer provided. No written prayer can address the thoughts, concerns, feelings, and inspirations that come up during the discussion.

If some group members already feel comfortable praying aloud in their own words, invite the group to join in the closing prayer right away. If not, wait a week or two. Once you feel that the group has the familiarity to prevent this from being too awkward, invite them to participate. You could tell the group that you will begin the closing prayer and then allow for a time of silence so that they can also pray aloud. Make sure they know that you will close the group's prayer by leading them into an Our Father after everyone is done praying spontaneously. This structure helps people feel that the time is contained and not completely lacking in structure. That helps free them to pray aloud.

Below are some possible ways to introduce your group to oral extemporaneous prayer. Don't read these suggestions verbatim—put them into your own words. It's not conducive to helping people become comfortable praying aloud spontaneously if you are reading out of a book!

*"The closing prayer is a great time to take the reflections we've shared, bring them to God, and ask him to help us make any inspirations a reality in our lives. God doesn't care about how well-spoken or articulate we are when we pray, so we shouldn't either! We don't judge each other's prayers. Let's just pray from our hearts, knowing that God hears and cares about what we say, not how perfectly we say it. When we pray something aloud, we know that the Holy Spirit is mightily at work within us because it's the Spirit who gives us the courage to speak."*

*"Tonight for the closing prayer, let's first each voice our needs to one another; then we will take turns putting our right hand on the shoulder of the person to the right of us and praying for that person. After we each express our prayer needs, I will start by praying for Karen on my right. That means that I need to listen carefully when she tells us what she needs prayer for. We may not remember everyone's needs, so be sure to listen well to the person on your right. I'll voice my prayer needs first; then we'll go around the circle to the right. Then I will begin with the Sign of the Cross and pray for _____ (name of person to the right) with my hand on his (or her) his shoulder. Okay? Does anyone have any questions?"*

## Connection to the Cross This Week

These weekly prayer and reflection exercises allow Jesus to enter more fully into the hearts of you and your small group members. If we don't give God the time that allows him to work in us, we experience far less fruit from our small group discussions. Prayer and reflection water the seeds that have been planted during the small group so that they can take root. Without the "water" of prayer and reflection, the sun will scorch the seed, and it will shrivel up and die, "since it had no root" (Mark 4:6). Encountering Christ during the week on our own makes it possible for us to be "rooted" in Christ (cf. Colossians 2:7) and to drink deeply of the "living water" (John 4:10) that he longs to pour into our souls.

Please review the "Connection to the Cross This Week" section in advance so that you're familiar with it, and then together as a group during each meeting. Reviewing it together will show everyone that it is an important part of the small group. Ask for feedback each week about how these prayer and reflection exercises are going. Don't spend too long on this topic, however, especially in the early weeks while members are still becoming comfortable together and growing more accustomed to praying on their own. Asking about their experience with the recommended prayer, sacrament, or spiritual exercise will help you know who is hungry for spiritual growth and who might need more encouragement. The witness of participants' stories from their times of prayer can ignite the interest of others who are less motivated to pray.

# About The Evangelical Catholic

The Evangelical Catholic (EC) equips Catholic ministries for evangelization by inspiring, training, and supporting local leaders to launch dynamic outreach. Through training events, services, and ongoing contractual relationships, the EC forms and trains Catholic pastoral staff and lay leaders for long-term evangelical efforts that can be locally sustained without ongoing site visits and regular consulting.

To accomplish this mission, we equip the lay faithful to invite the lost into the joy of life in Christ and stem the tide of Catholics leaving the Church. We form pastoral staff to make disciples, shepherd evangelistic ministries, and manage pastoral structure to make discipleship to Jesus the natural outcome within the parish or university campus ministry

Our prayer is that through the grace of the Holy Spirit, we can help make the Church's mission of evangelization accessible, natural, and fruitful for every Catholic, and that many lives will be healed and transformed by knowing Jesus within the Church.